PRAISE FOR
The Power
of Mindful Learning

"*The Power of Mindful Learning* argues that traditional methods of learning can produce mindless behavior because they tend to get people to 'overlearn' a fact or a task and suggest that there is only one way to do it. She argues that it is important to teach skills and facts conditionally, setting the stage for doubt and an awareness that different situations may call for different approaches or answers....Landmark studies make the point scientifically."   —*The New York Times*

"Like Freud, Piaget, Werner, and Vygotsky, Langer is well on her way to constructing a grand theory of human functioning with important implications for such diverse areas as education and learning, development and aging, group relations, and psycho- and neuro-pathology....Never before has social psychology provided more subtle insights into neuropsychology and related fields than in Langer's provocative work....Her seemingly simple experimental manipulations point out profound truths about the human condition and how we as people can develop."   —Edith Kaplan
Contemporary Psychology

"Many educators find her theory intriguing and think it has profound implications for revolutionizing teaching at all levels."
—*APA Monitor*

"Most of us are often mindless in our learning. How this happens and what can be done about it—these are Ellen Langer's important questions. Her lively answers could radically change our concept of learning."

—Jerome Bruner
The New School for Social Research

"A wonderfully thoughtful and thought-provoking follow-up to the author's earlier study *Mindfulness*, this time exploring the ill effects of mindlessness in education....An excellent introduction to what might be (and certainly should be) the next paradigm shift in education."

—*Kirkus Reviews*

"An interesting and very readable proposal...Each of the seven chapters takes up a learning 'myth'...to reduce the mindlessness pervasive in traditional education."

—*Choice*

"I'm a firm believer in the power of mindful learning. This book should be required reading for teachers at every level, both in academia and the business world."

—Howard Stevenson
Harvard Business School

The Power
of Mindful Learning

The Power
of Mindful
Learning

Ellen J. Langer

A MERLOYD LAWRENCE BOOK
LIFELONG BOOKS ● DA CAPO PRESS
A Member of the Perseus Books Group

Cataloging-in-Publication Data is available from the Library of Congress.

Da Capo Press is a member of the Perseus Books Group.

Find us on the World Wide Web at
http://www.dacapopress.com

Perseus Publishing books are available for special discounts for bulk purchases in the U.S. by corporations, institutions, and other organizations. For more information, please contact the Special Markets Department at Perseus Books Group, 11Cambridge Center, Cambridge, MA 02142, or call 1-800-255-1514 or email Special.Markets@perseusbooks.com.

Text design by Dede Cummings
Set in 11 pt Caslon by A&B Typesetters

05 06   20 19 18 17 16

Contents

Acknowledgments *xi*

INTRODUCTION   1

1 WHEN PRACTICE MAKES IMPERFECT   9
Overlearned Skills   11
Whose Basics?   15
The Value of Doubt   15
Sideways Learning   22
Can a Text Teach Mindfully?   28

2 CREATIVE DISTRACTION   33
The Puzzle of "Attention"   37
Enhancing Novelty   40
Soft Vigilance   43
Rethinking Attention Deficit Hyperactivity Disorder   44

3 THE MYTH OF DELAYED GRATIFICATION   51
All Work and No Play   52
Turning Play into Work   56
Turning Work into Play   58

CONTENTS

4 1066 WHAT? OR THE HAZARDS OF ROTE MEMORY   67

Locking Up Information   69

Keeping Information Available   73

Drawing Distinctions   75

5 A NEW LOOK AT FORGETTING   83

Staying in the Present   85

The Dangers of Mindless Memory   87

Absentminded versus Other Minded?   89

Does Memory Decline?   90

Alternative Views of Memory and Aging   93

6 MINDFULNESS AND INTELLIGENCE   99

Nineteenth-Century Theories of Intelligence   102

The Notion of Optimum Fit   106

An Alternative Ability   107

Linear versus Mindful Problem Solving   111

7 THE ILLUSION OF RIGHT ANSWERS   117

Hobbled by Outcomes   120

Actor/Observer and Other Perspectives   122

Uncertainty and Creative Thought   129

When Right Becomes Wrong   132

Mindfulness and Self-Definition   135

Learning as Re-imagining the World   137

Notes 141

Index 157

About the Author 169

Acknowledgments

Each chapter of this book relies in part on the mindfulness of various students with whom I've had the pleasure of working. Their contributions are noted throughout where our experiments are described. Even more extensive collaboration and thus special thanks are extended to Douglas DeMay and Paul Whitmore re chapter 1; to Mathew Lieberman re chapter 4; Becca Levy re chapter 5; and Justin Brown re our work on intelligence.

Taken as a whole, this book has benefited greatly from the comments and questions given to me by Roger Brown and Lenore Weitzman. Katherine Jaeger, Trina Soske, John Myers, Albert Carnasale, Marie Tatar, Phyllis Katz, and Nancy Hemenway also provided useful insights. I extend my gratitude to each for their advice and my appreciation of their friendship.

I also want to thank Sophia Snow and Brian Ericcson for their mindful technical help.

ACKNOWLEDGMENTS

Last, but foremost, I am indebted to my editor and friend, Merloyd Lawrence, whose skill, patience, and wisdom helped me with each draft.

The Power
of Mindful Learning

Introduction

Once upon a time there was a mindless little girl named Little Red Riding Hood. One day, when she went to visit her ailing grandmother, she was greeted by a wolf dressed in her grandmother's nightclothes. "What big eyes you have, Grandma," she exclaimed, clueless as ever, although she had seen her grandmother's eyes countless times before. "What big ears you have, Grandma," she said, although it was unlikely that they would have changed since her last visit. "What a deep voice you have, Grandma," she said, still oblivious to the shaggy imposter beneath the familiar lacy nightcap. "What big teeth you have," she said, too late, alas, to begin paying attention.

Certain myths and fairy tales help advance a culture by passing on a profound and complex wisdom to succeeding generations. Others, however, deserve to be questioned. This book is about seven pervasive myths, or mindsets, that undermine the process of learning and how we can avoid their debilitating effects in a wide variety of settings.

1. The basics must be learned so well that they become second nature.
2. Paying attention means staying focused on one thing at a time.
3. Delaying gratification is important.
4. Rote memorization is necessary in education.
5. Forgetting is a problem.
6. Intelligence is knowing "what's out there."
7. There are right and wrong answers.

These myths undermine true learning. They stifle our creativity, silence our questions, and diminish our self-esteem. Throughout this book we will examine them, sometimes through experiments carried out at Harvard and elsewhere and sometimes with insight drawn from fairy tales and folktales from around the world. The process of overturning these myths leads to certain questions about the nature of intelligence. In the last two chapters we will explore these questions and the ways in which our view of intelligence may support inhibiting mindsets.

The ideas offered here to loosen the grip of these debilitating myths are very simple. Their fundamental simplicity points to yet another inhibiting myth: that only a massive overhaul can give us a more effective educational system.

We can change school curricula, change standards for testing students and teachers, increase parent and community involvement in the process of education, and increase the budget for education so that more students can become part of the computer age. None of these measures alone will make enough difference unless students are given the opportunity to learn more mindfully. With such opportunity, some of these expensive measures might well become unnecessary.

Wherever learning takes place—in school, on the job, in the home—these myths are also at work and the opportunity for mindful learning is present. Whether the learning is practical or theoretical, personal or interpersonal; whether it involves abstract concepts, such as physics, or concrete skills, such as how to play a sport, the way the information is learned will determine how, why, and when it is used. The succeeding chapters explore the way each of these myths locks us into rigid habits of learning and offer keys to a more flexible and productive approach.

This book takes more of a "why-to" than a "how-to" approach. Nevertheless, the examples and experiments described implicitly suggest ways to learn mindfully. These are intended to guide our choices and to be adapted to each unique context, rather than to be followed mindlessly.

Not only do we as individuals get locked into single-minded views, but we also reinforce these views for each other until the culture itself suffers the same mindlessness. There is an awareness of this in science. Scientists proceed along a path gathering data that builds on accepted wisdom. At some point someone turns everyone's attention to a very different view of the previously acknowledged truth. This phenomenon happens frequently enough that scientists are generally not surprised by what is called a paradigm shift. In a recent *New York Times*[1] article psychologist Dean Radin described four stages of adopting ideas: "The first is, 1. 'It's impossible.' 2. 'Maybe it's possible, but it's weak and uninteresting.' 3. 'It is true and I told you so.' 4. 'I thought of it first.' " I would add a fifth stage, "We always knew that. How could it be otherwise?"

The term *mindful learning* is used here in a very specific way, drawn from the concept of mindfulness that I defined in an earlier book by that name.[2] A mindful approach to any activity has three characteristics: the continuous creation of new categories; openness to new information; and an implicit awareness of more than one perspective. Mindlessness, in contrast, is characterized by an entrapment in old categories; by automatic behavior that precludes attending to new signals; and by action that operates from a single perspective. Being mindless, colloquially speaking, is like being on automatic pilot. In *Mindfulness*, I described the benefits of a mindful approach for our psychological and physical well-being. For instance, elderly adults given mindfulness treatments were shown to live longer than their peers who were not given such treatments. In this book I use the concept of mindfulness as a lens through which to explore its importance in the world I know best, teaching and learning.

In many of my classes students are quick to point out examples of their own and others' mindlessness. The examples often come from the texts and research under discussion. When I'm the perpetrator of this mindlessness, I examine it closely. Why didn't I reconsider the old information when presenting it in a new context? Why did I trot out the received wisdom on this particular topic? Such puzzles keep sending me back to investigate the way I learned the information in the first place.

Each year, in a course I teach on decision making and perceived control, to bounce my students out of their habitual state of mind I ask them if one can prevent pregnancy with a nasal spray. They laugh or at least grimace at this obvious absurdity. Then I show them what by now is an old newspaper article with the headline "Nasal spray as a new means of birth control," and their interest picks up. Their first response is not unusual. When faced with something that hasn't been done before, people frequently express the belief that it can't be done. All progress, of course, depends on questioning that belief. *Everything is the same until it is not.* If instead of asking, "Is it possible to prevent pregnancy with a nasal spray?" we ask, "How could we use a nasal spray as a method of birth control?" we set off on a different search, in a different frame of mind. Instead of dismissing the question as foolish, we start thinking about how to get from the nose to the egg and sperm. Once we generate possible ways of doing something, even if they are low-probability bets, the perception of a solution's being possible increases enormously. (I may have to come up with a new puzzle next semester, since recent research on pheromones and their influence on hormone levels has made a nasal contraceptive seem less incredible.)

Although with a range of ability and accomplishments, the students I meet are among the brightest imaginable. Yet even the very best can be mindless, insecure about what they know. Ironically, many are unhappy with an educational experience that has only rewarded them. Their dissatisfaction may result from certain of these debilitating myths, such as that expressed in "Study now, play later." Throughout their careers, these gifted students have learned to delay gratification. Why is study itself not gratifying? If not, how could it be? If rote memory is a tedious way to prepare for an exam, is there a more effective and more gratifying way?

These students have all been tested, tried, and found to be worthy of extreme praise. What does it mean when such an intelligent person gives a wrong answer? Is the wrong answer a lapse, an indication of stupidity? Or does the "wrong" answer merit consideration? And if for these students, why not for all students?

In trying to answer these questions I will not limit the notion of learning to the classroom. In our so-called learning society the mindsets that hobble us can be found all over: from music lessons to investment analysis; from television viewing to psychotherapy. As we will see, our attitudes toward aging and advertising, our approach to decisions, and even our preferences in art, sports, or entertainment all depend on the views we hold about the nature of learning. As an example, a very intelligent friend of mine, successful in business, was told, to her dismay, that she had an attention problem. I was surprised. I burrowed into the vast literature on attention deficit hyperactivity disorder (ADHD), read the symptoms of the disorder, and was even more surprised to see that I have it as well. Or do I? What exactly does it mean to pay attention? We have to answer this question before we can sensibly talk about a deficit or disability.

From questions such as these I was drawn into a more general investigation of education and how we learn. By observation and experiment, I have come to see how seven particular myths make it hard to learn and in the process, make it hard to teach.

1

When Practice Makes Imperfect

When he arrived on the planet he respectfully saluted the lamplighter.

"Good morning. Why have you just put out your lamp?"

"These are the instructions," replied the lamplighter. "Good morning."

"What are the instructions?"

"The instructions are that I put out my lamp. Good evening."

And he lighted his lamp again.

"But why have you just lighted it again?"

"These are the instructions," replied the lamplighter.

"I do not understand," said the little prince.

"There is nothing to understand," said the lamplighter. "Instructions are instructions. Good morning."

And he put out his lamp.

Then he mopped his forehead with a handkerchief decorated with red squares.

"I follow a terrible profession. In the old days it was reasonable. I put the lamp out in the morning and in the evening I lighted it again. I had the rest of the day for relaxation and the rest of the night for sleep."

"And the instructions have been changed since that time?"

"The instructions have not been changed," said the lamplighter. "That is the tragedy! From year to year the planet has turned more rapidly and the orders have not been changed!"

The Little Prince
ANTOINE DE SAINT-EXUPÉRY[1]

Day after day the celestial lamplighter performed his well-practiced task. For him by now it was second nature. The planet, however, like the rest of the world, kept on changing. The routine stayed fixed, while the context changed.

One of the most cherished myths in education or any kind of training is that in order to learn a skill one must practice it to the point of doing it without thinking. Whether I ask colleagues concerned with higher education, parents of young children, or students themselves, everyone seems to agree on this approach to what are called the basics. Whether it is learning how to play baseball, drive, or teach, the advice is the same: practice the basics until they become second nature. I think this is the wrong way to start.

OVERLEARNED SKILLS

Before explaining this last statement, let me give an example of just one context for each of the skills I mentioned that might lead one to question this faith in practicing the basics.

As a child in summer camp I was taught to practice holding a baseball bat a particular way. The idea was to do so without thinking so that I could attend to other aspects of the game, such as the particular pitch I was trying to hit. Now, after years of lifting weights imperfectly, my right arm is stronger than my left. Should I hold the bat the same way in spite of this difference? Should everyone hold a bat the same way?

Because my driving skills have been overlearned, I flip my turn signal on automatically before making a turn. Now, suppose that I'm on an icy road about to make a turn, but the car is somewhat out of control. Wouldn't turning on the signal in the same old way misguide the car behind me by seeming to indicate that the situation is well in hand? Would use of the flashing light be more appropriate in this context? Recently I gave a talk in New Mexico. I was driven from the airport to the hotel across a desert, without a car in sight for miles and miles. At each turn, the driver dutifully signaled.

Imagine overlearning the basics of driving in the United States and then taking a vacation in London, where people drive on the left side of the road. The car in front of you swerves out of control and you must react quickly. Do you slip back to old habits or avoid an accident by responding to what the current situation demands? It is interesting to consider that emergencies may often be the result of actions taken in response to previous training rather than in response to present considerations.

One of the "basic skills" of teachers, and all lecturers, is the ability to take a large quantity of information and present it in bite-size pieces to students. For those of us who teach, reducing and organizing information becomes second nature. How often do we, so practiced in how to prepare information for a lecture, continue to present a prepared lesson without noticing that the class is no longer paying attention? Presenting all the prepared content too often overtakes the goal of teaching.

For students, note-taking skills can be overlearned, practiced as second nature. Many of us have had the experience of turning to our notes and finding that we don't have the vaguest idea what they mean.

Traveling makes us particularly aware of rigidities. In several Asian countries drivers drive on the left side of the road, and pedestrians on the busy sidewalks follow the same pattern as cars, staying to the right or left accordingly. The frequency with which I came close to walking into people when traveling in Asia made clear to me that even a simple exercise, such as walking on the right, if originally learned mindlessly, may be hard to change. Each time I traveled to a different country, the rules changed, and my awkwardness increased.

In an art gallery in Hanoi, I encountered the results of basic training in Western customs of politeness. The gallery owner offered me a seat from which to view the paintings. I politely refused. She offered it to me three more times. It appeared that her lesson did not include what to do if the customer preferred to stand. She took her cues as to what to do from her lesson, and not from the situation.

In Singapore, on my way to Chinatown, I asked the taxi driver how large the Chinese population was. He answered, "Seventy-six percent of the country is Chinese." I said, "Are you sure it's not 77 percent?" He laughed, although I think many would not have been sure what I was getting at. The government had published a report saying that 76 percent of the population was Chinese, and for many that remained fact without any awareness that births, deaths, emigrations, or immigrations could change the number at any moment. This is the way most of us have been taught to take in information—as though it is true irrespective of new contexts.

When we drill ourselves in a certain skill so that it becomes second nature, does this lead to performing the skill mindlessly? Do we set limits on ourselves by practicing to the point of overlearning? When we approach a new skill, whether as adults or children, it is, by definition, a time when we know the least about it. Does it make sense to freeze our understanding of the skill before we try it out in different contexts and, at various stages, adjust it to our own strengths and experiences? Does it make sense to stick to what we first learned when that learning occurred when we were most naive? When we first learn a skill, we necessarily attend to each individual step. If we overlearn the drill, we essentially lose sight of the individual components and we find it hard to make small adjustments.

Learning the basics in a rote, unthinking manner almost ensures mediocrity. At the least, it deprives learners of maximizing their own potential for more effective performance and, as we will see in Chapter 3, for enjoyment of the activity. Consider tennis. At tennis camp I was taught exactly how to hold my racket and toss the ball when serving. We were all taught the same way. When I later watched the U.S. Open, I noticed that none of the top players served the way I was taught, and, more important, each of them served slightly differently. Most of us are not taught our skills, whether academic, athletic, or artistic, by the real experts. The rules we are given to practice are based on generally accepted truths about how to perform the task and not on our individual abilities. If we mindlessly practice these skills, we are not likely to surpass our teachers. Even if we are fortunate enough to be shown how to do something by a true expert, mindless practice keeps the activity from becoming our own. If I try to serve exactly as Martina Navratilova serves, will I be as good as she (apart from differences in innate gifts), given that my grip of the racket is determined by my hand size, not hers, and my toss of the ball is affected by my height, not hers, and given the differences in our muscles? Each difference between me and my instructor could be a problem if I take each instruction for granted. If we learn the basics but do not overlearn them, we can vary them as we change or as the situation changes.

WHOSE BASICS?

Perhaps the very notion of basics needs to be questioned. So-called basic skills are normatively derived. They are usually at least partially applicable for most people some of the time. They are sometimes not useful at all for some people (e.g., how to hold the racket for someone who is missing a finger or how to read a text for someone with dyslexia). They are not useful, however, as first learned, for everyone across all situations. If they are mindlessly overlearned, they are not likely to be varied even when variation would be advantageous. Perhaps one could say that for everyone there are certain basics, but that there is no such thing as *the* basics.

In the classroom, teaching one set of basics for everyone may appear to be easier for the teacher because the teacher needs to know less, a single routine leaves little room for disagreement and hence may foster obedience to authority, and it seems impossible to give individualized training to several people at once.

There are ways, however, to foster mindful learning of basic skills in classrooms full of potential experts. The rationale for this change in approaches is based on the belief that experts at anything become expert in part by varying those same basics. The rest of us, taught not to question, take them for granted.

THE VALUE OF DOUBT

The key to this new way of teaching is based on an appreciation of both the conditional, or context-dependent, nature of the world and the value of uncertainty. Teaching skills and facts in a conditional way sets the stage for doubt and an awareness of how different situations may call for subtle differences in what we bring to them. This way of teaching imposes no special burden on teachers. Rather, it may increase their own mindfulness as it helps individual students come closer to realizing their potential.

Consider an example that may seem trivial at first, yet speaks to how difficult it is to change what we have mindlessly learned. At a friend's house for dinner I noticed that the table was set with the fork on the right side of the plate. Of course, being polite, I said nothing, although I felt as though some natural order had been violated. I couldn't seem to dismiss the thought that the fork goes on the left side of the plate, even though I was aware that the feeling was preposterous. I even felt that it made more sense in some ways for the fork to reside where my friend had placed it, given that most people in this country would retrieve it with the right hand. Where did my mindset come from? My mother taught me how to set the table when I was young. Her view was not discussed. It was not made into a big deal. It was simply stated, and I mindlessly learned it.

To linger in the kitchen a moment longer, consider how many people cook. Having once been taught when and how to use certain ingredients and spices it occurs to few of us to change recipes to accommodate changes in age, minor health problems, seasons, and the like. Yet unintentional changes sometimes bring about useful learning.

Once a year I attempt to bake. I have a wonderful recipe for marble cheesecake, which I appear to be unable to ruin. The first time I made it I put it in the oven for a few minutes and then realized I had forgotten to add the heavy cream. I took it out of the oven and added the cream. The next time I used light cream, followed by half-and-half on the next occasion, with perfectly acceptable results. When I add the chocolate, for some reason the cake ends up speckled instead of marbled. Never having learned how to bake, I didn't see these deviations from the recipe as a disaster. I simply changed the name of the cake so it is not an inferior marble cheesecake. This no-fault cheesecake always tastes delicious to me because I use only ingredients I like, but more important, I enjoy varying it rather than mindlessly following an unconditional recipe.

Most of what we learn in school, at home, from television, and from nonfiction books we may mindlessly accept because it is given to us in an unconditional form. That is, the information is presented from a single perspective as though it is true, independent of context. It just *is*. Typically, no uncertainty is conveyed. Much of what we know about the world, about other people, and about ourselves is usually processed in this same way.

We can learn a skill by accepting at face value what we are told about how to practice it or we can come to an understanding over time of what the skill entails. Even in the latter case, we eventually try to get the skill down pat. In research Lois Imber and I conducted many years ago, we found that when people overlearn a task so that they can perform it by rote, the individual steps that make up the skill come together into larger and larger units.[2] As a consequence, the smaller components of the activity are essentially lost, yet it is by adjusting and varying these pieces that we can improve our performance.

Recently, with students Dina Dudkin, Diana Brandt, ar.d Todd Bodner, I set out to test more directly the idea that teaching material conditionally allows students to manipulate the information creatively in a different context. Some ways of teaching conditionally may be surprisingly simple.

In a pilot experiment, high school students with the same basic experience and education were taught a lesson in physics.[3] The lesson was on videotape, and all the students saw the same videotape. Before viewing the tape, however, half the students received an instruction sheet informing them that their participation consisted of two parts: "Part I consists of a 30-minute video that will introduce a few basic concepts of physics. Part II involves a short questionnaire in which you will apply the concepts shown in the video. The video presents only one of several outlooks on physics, which may or may not be helpful to you. Please feel free to use any additional methods you want to assist you in solving the problems." The other half of the group was told the same thing but with no mention of several outlooks or of additional methods. Our hypothesis was that the instruction to allow for alternatives would encourage mindful learning.

On direct tests of the material, the groups performed equally well. For questions that required students to extrapolate beyond the information given, to use it creatively, a different picture is emerging. Although nothing in either the video or the instructions forbade using previous knowledge and experience to help solve these problems, only the students given the mindful instructions tended to do so. Students who were not given these instructions were the only ones to complain about the material. Although it is too early in this investigation to be sure of the results (a situation of mindful uncertainty), a prior study done with Alison Piper, described fully in *Mindfulness,* suggests there is merit in this approach.[4] In that study students were introduced to a set of objects either conditionally ("This could be a . . .") or in absolute form ("This is a . . ."). As in the pilot study just described, we tested to see whether conditional information allowed for alternatives. We found that only those students taught conditionally thought to use the objects in creative ways.

Another way of presenting information mindfully makes use of students' mindlessness. This approach was suggested to me by Jerry Avorn of Harvard Medical School. In a lecture given to our department he told of a drug that was tested in a randomized clinical study. Patients were given either the drug or a placebo, an inert substance, and did not know which they were given. On the chalkboard during his lecture Avorn put a list of side effects, such as nausea, headaches, and fatigue, and wrote rather high percentages next to each. Seeing the list, we all assumed that this was a rather risky treatment, only to find out that the numbers corresponded to the placebo group.

In a similar way information, be it from psychology or history, can be presented with figures for the main variables reversed, and students can be asked to come up with explanations for these "facts." We're all very good at working backward and coming up with reasons to justify any opinion. In so doing we often box ourselves into a single view. I find that as students generate more and more reasons, they become more likely to believe that the "fact" is true. The more we think this way in or out of the classroom, the more we are likely to believe in one right answer. In the classroom, when I reveal that the fact is actually the opposite of what I presented, the students seem to get the point without further discussion. The more often we learn the basics with the recognition, from the start, that there are several, perhaps quite disparate ways of accounting for information, the more open we are to alternatives.

To make this point clearer, consider a presentation of the classic Milgram study on obedience to authority (to students who aren't familiar with it).[5] In this study subjects played the part of a teacher. They were instructed to administer shocks to a learner whenever he made an error. Unbeknownst to the subjects, the learner was a confederate of the experimenter; despite his cries with every supposed shock, he felt no pain. The shocks appeared to increase in intensity, and subjects were instructed to continue even though the shocks might actually kill the learner. A certain percentage of the subjects obeyed the experimenter and administered the most intense level of shock. In discussing this study for teaching purposes, I make two columns on the chalkboard: percentage of those who fully obeyed and percentage of those who did not. In the first column I write 35 percent and in the second, 65 percent. Students generate explanations for why most people did not obey and I should add, they do so with great certainty: "People don't like to be pushed around," "People are compassionate and don't want to see anyone suffer," and so on. At this point I turn to the board and notice that I "mislabeled" the columns.

Gender differences may also be a factor in whether new skills are learned in an absolute or conditional manner. Lori Pietrasz and I conducted a study to explore this question.[6] We hypothesized that one reason males typically outperform females on athletic tasks might be a difference in the way they process instructions. In general young girls are taught to be "good little girls" which translates into "do what you are told." To be a "real boy," on the other hand, implicitly means to be independent of authority and "don't listen to all you are told." This difference should be especially salient in sex-typed activities such as sports. Our hypothesis was that motivation to be a good girl would lead to taking in information about the basics in an absolute or mindless way. Similarly, being a bit rebellious was expected to result in conditional or mindful learning.

To eliminate much previous learning, participants were instructed in how to play a novel game: Smack-it ball. The game is similar to squash except that a small racket that fits like a baseball mitt is worn on both hands. Half of the males and half of the females were instructed in how to use the rackets either in conditional or absolute language (eg. "one way to hold your hand might be . . ." vs "this is how to hold your hand"). After practicing the game, we surreptitiously changed the ball to one that was quite a bit heavier and thus required different body movements. We noted performance at this time. It was expected that the instructions would not differentiate the male groups because they were assumed to conditionalize the instructions no matter how they were given by us. Females on the other hand were expected to be trapped by their original learning—when taught in an absolute manner—and not to adjust to the changed circumstances (the heavier ball). Thus their performance should be inferior to that of those taught in a conditional way. The findings confirmed our expectations. Moreover, when females were taught conditionally their performance was not different from their male counterparts.

It is interesting to consider other sex-typed tasks from this perspective. While girls outperform boys in early math classes, the reverse typically becomes the case in late high school and college. Much of what we are taught about math initally has to be amended as we approach more advanced topics. Initially there are numbers; later we find out that there are prime numbers, irrational numbers, different number systems, etc. The more rigidly we learn the original information, the harder it may be to open up those closed packages to accommodate the new information. "Good girls" learn the basics in an absolute way from the teacher/authority.

SIDEWAYS LEARNING

The standard two approaches to teaching new skills are top-down or bottom-up. The top-down method relies on discursive lecturing to instruct students. The bottom-up path relies on direct experience, repeated practice of the new activity in a systematic way. Although both approaches have their advocates, I sought a third alternative. Rather than imposing an order from above or repetitively indoctrinating students through practice, my students and I investigated the effectiveness of activities that break with these two traditions. This approach could be called sideways learning. My no-fault cheesecake is an instance of sideways learning. The basics of cheesecake making were repeatedly varied, serving as a rough guide for making the cake rather than a rigid formula.

Sideways learning aims at maintaining a mindful state. As we saw, the concept of mindfulness revolves around certain psychological states that are really different versions of the same thing: (1) openness to novelty; (2) alertness to distinction; (3) sensitivity to different contexts; (4) implicit, if not explicit, awareness of multiple perspectives; and (5) orientation in the present.[7] Each leads to the others and back to itself. Learning a subject or skill with an openness to novelty and actively noticing differences, contexts, and perspectives—sideways learning— makes us receptive to changes in an ongoing situation. In such a state of mind, basic skills and information guide our behavior in the present, rather than run it like a computer program.

Mindfulness creates a rich awareness of discriminatory detail. Theories that suggest that we learn best when we break a task down into discrete parts do not really make possible the sort of learning that is accomplished through mindful awareness of distinctions. Getting our experience presliced undermines the opportunity to reach mindful awareness. Sideways learning, however, involves attending to multiple ways of carving up the same domain. It not only makes it possible to create unlimited categories and distinctions to differentiate one task from another, but it is essential to mobilizing mindfulness.

Can novices be jostled into mindful awareness? How can a situation release our full mental resources and increase our ability to learn and retain complex skills? One pilot study (discussed later) suggests that expertise is not dependent on a particular hierarchical assimilation of basic skills, but that greater effectiveness and mastery may be accessible through inventive transformations of the routine.

Much traditional training, such as developed and organized training in classical piano, leads many people to believe that technique is identical to the internalization of some set of rules for correct performance. Yet the observations of critics evaluating a performer often raise questions about this assumption.

Certain players seem almost exclusively absorbed in the action of their fingers over the piano keys, as if forgetting how the rest of the body participates in playing and contributes to the support of the hands. If a pianist is preoccupied with the voluntary, manipulable end of the spectrum of neurological possibilities, this preoccupation resounds in the music. The performance sounds calculated, not shaped from a spontaneous response. Hence critics often comment on virtuosos who, for all their technical brilliance, are unfeeling, or mechanical, or characterless, and so on. Walter Gieseking, a well-known German pianist, asked his students to learn the music away from the piano, so as to do away altogether with attention to technique and correctness.

In such players there may be a lack of smooth coordination between agile hands and a motionless or inexpressive trunk. The energy generated for striking the keys is isolated.[8] In a truly great performance all technical skills are transformed into a unique, context-sensitive, one-of-a-kind experience. This raises the question of whether technique, assimilated through hours of drill, is the essential or even the primary ingredient of mastery.

Expertise, of course, involves several dimensions. First, some element of genetic endowment may differentiate initial aptitude. Animals are born with the ability to walk and quickly manage to accomplish complex tasks requiring balance, acute perception, or navigational ability, a feat that humans could never emulate. Among humans, the existence of prodigies in domains such as music, mathematics, and chess indicates that the initial mental organization of some individuals can predispose them to rapid and relatively untutored mastery.[9] To explore approaches to learning basic skills, it is necessary to look at skills that are more generally spread across the population, leaving aside the possibility that the truly gifted are different from the rest of us in ways genetically determined.

Clearly, some experience is necessary to acquire complex skills. Yet imagine a coach or piano teacher prescribing a set amount of practice, every day. To claim that any particular amount of time on a task is sufficient to learn that skill overlooks the state in which such practice is approached. How much piano, or golf, or tennis can one learn while daydreaming about some other activity? Pressed to its logical extreme, this teaching method would rely solely on moving the body, with the assumption that the mind would follow. If so, one could learn while asleep simply by having one's body moved in the proper patterns.

Although certain therapies have actually made use of some version of this mode (body therapies or neurolinguistic programming), full mastery is not their goal. Recognizing the difference between going through the motions and moving one's body in awareness brings us into the domain of mindfulness.

J.R. Anderson has described three stages of experience that result in the acquisition of a new skill.[10] The *cognitive* stage involves first taking in enough information about the skill to permit the learner to perform the desired behavior in at least some crude approximation. This stage often involves self-talk, in which the learner rehearses information required to carry out the skill. The *associative* stage involves smoothing out performance. Any errors in the initial understanding of the skill are gradually identified and eliminated in this stage, and at the same time there is a drop in self-talk. The *autonomous* stage is one of ongoing gradual improvement in performance. In this stage improvement can continue indefinitely.

Paul Whitmore, Douglas DeMay, and I investigated whether learning can in fact be improved by changing the mode of the initial learning, the cognitive stage. In a small study, novice piano players were introduced to a simple C-major scale under two conditions, explicitly mindful or traditional practice. People were recruited for the study through flyers announcing a free piano lesson. They were randomly assigned to one of two groups. All subjects were given essentially the same instruction in piano, with the following variations. Members of group 1, the mindful instruction group, were instructed to be creative and to vary their playing as much as possible. These subjects were told: "We would like you to try to learn these fingering exercises without relying on rote memorization. Try to keep learning new things about your piano playing. Try to change your style every few minutes, and not lock into one particular pattern. While you practice, attend to the context, which may include very subtle variations or any feelings, sensations, or thoughts you are having." Halfway through the session they were reminded to try to keep learning new things, to change the approach every few minutes, and not to lock into any single pattern. Then the specific lesson was given, and subjects spent twenty minutes practicing it. The control group was taught to practice in a more traditional, memorization-through-repetition style.

The piano playing was taped for evaluation. Two graduate students in music who had extensive keyboarding and compositional experience rated the playing. In addition, subjects were asked how well they liked the lessons. The findings of this study confirmed our hypotheses. In comparison with the control group, the subjects given mindful instruction in the early steps of piano playing were rated as more competent and more creative and also expressed more enjoyment of the activity.

Many keyboard masters played the organ while becoming expert on the piano. Mozart, Beethoven, Schumann, and Glenn Gould, for example, recommended organ practice to achieve greater clarity in composing and playing the piano.[11] Yehudi Menuhin said he thought his violin playing improved after he took up the viola. To play two similiar but different instruments at once works against taking one set of basic skills for granted and thereby encourages an alert and mindful state. An awareness of alternatives at the early stages of learning a skill gives a conditional quality to the learning, which, again, increases mindfulness.

CAN A TEXT TEACH MINDFULLY?

Because a lot of learning takes place not from exercises planned by an individual teacher but from a textbook, the question arises whether a textbook can inform mindfully.

Todd Bodner, Randy Waterfield, and I tested the hypothesis that with slight modifications textbooks could encourage creative use of learned material.[12] We chose a learning situation that has broad implications for the world of finance. The Series 7 Examination is an exam that every stockbroker, indeed, nearly every person who wants to be involved in investment-related employment, must pass. It is the equivalent of the bar exam in law and carries with it similar stress and concern for a passing grade. It is a comprehensive test intended to protect the investors from people who are not competent to advise them.

We obtained a copy of the Series 7 preparation and testing materials and chose a twelve-page chapter to rewrite. Our selection was guided by two criteria: first, the material had to be obscure enough that our research participants would be unfamiliar with it, and second, understanding the material had to be crucial to passing the test. The chapter was rewritten so that all statements originally expressed in absolute terms now conveyed a more conditional meaning. For example, the original text read,

"Municipal bonds are issued by states, territories, and possessions of the United States, as well as other political subdivisions. Such political subdivisions would include counties, cities, special districts for schools, waterworks, sewers. Public agencies such as authorities and commissions also issue municipal bonds.") The more conditionally written text reads: "In most cases, municipal bonds are issued by states, territories, and possessions of the United States, as well as other political subdivisions. Such political subdivisions may include counties, cities, special districts for schools, waterworks, sewers, and other public purposes that may require the issuance of municipal bonds. Public agencies such as authorities and commissions may on occasion issue municipal bonds for a wide variety of public projects in addition to those mentioned above." As another example, the original text read, "For local jurisdictions such as cities, the most common taxing power is on property. An *ad valorem* tax on the assessed value of real estate is the source of funds the local government uses to support its expenses and debt (GO bonds). School taxes are also charged at the local level." The mindful text read, "For local jurisdictions, which could be counties and cities, the most common taxing power may be on property. An *ad valorem* tax on the assessed value of real estate is probably the source of funds the local government uses most often to support its expenses and debt (GO bonds). Of course, there are other ways a local jurisdiction can obtain money, one of which is through school taxes."

Harvard undergraduate students served as subjects. They were randomly divided into two groups. Half received the original version of the material, and half received the more conditional version. Students studied the material for twenty-five minutes and then took a two-part test. The first part tested creative use of the learned material. The second part tested students' grasp of the factual material through a multiple-choice format. In addition, we asked questions to determine whether the students liked the material they studied.

In the test of creative use of the material, students were asked, for example, to "write as many different purposes for municipal bonds that you can think of." The multiple-choice test asked such routine factual questions as "Which of the following supplies money to a local jurisdiction? (a) *ad valorem* taxes; (b) school taxes; (c) parking tickets; (d) a & b; (e) a, b, & c."

Both groups performed similarly on direct tests of the material, but when creative use of the information was required, subjects who had studied from the mindful text clearly outperformed the other group. For our first example, for instance, students who had read the mindful text supplied six answers, whereas those who had read the original gave only four. For the tax question, 100 percent of the group instructed mindfully gave the correct answer (e), whereas only 36 percent of the other group answered correctly. In addition to outperforming the comparison group on the questions requiring some creative use of the information, the mindful learning group tended to like the material more.

To consider another example, imagine reading a programmed text on cardiopulmonary resuscitation (CPR). In very small steps, one by one, it teaches you how to rescue an adult. You've got it down pat. Another part just as methodically teaches you how to rescue an infant. You know all the required steps. A week after reading the text you are at a friend's pool when her seven-year-old daughter gets in over her head and needs CPR. There's not much time. What do you do? Now imagine that you learned each step of the original lesson conditionally, that is, with a sense that it might have to be adapted rather than as mindlessly sequential. Contrast your quandary in these two cases. You might now be better prepared to adjust to this new situation and more adequately adapt the steps to suit a fifty-pound child. Which way would you want to learn the lesson? How should we teach it?

2

Creative Distraction

In Switzerland there was once an old count. He had an only son, who couldn't seem to learn a thing. The father said: "Listen, my son. I've tried and tried, but I can't drum anything into your head. You will have to go away. I'm sending you to a famous teacher; let him see what he can do with you." The boy was sent to a strange city, and spent a whole year with the teacher. Then he returned home, and his father asked him: "Well, my son, what have you learned?" "Father," he replied, "I've learned what dogs say when they bark." "Heaven help us!" the father cried. "Is that all you've learned? I'll have to send you to another teacher." After a year the boy returned home. "Well, my son, what have you learned?" "Father, I've learned what the birds say." The father flew into a rage. "You good for nothing!" he cried, "wasting all that precious time and learning nothing. I'm going to send you to a third teacher and if you don't learn something this time, I won't be your father any more." When the son returned home his father asked him: "My son, what have you learned?" He replied: "Dear father, this year I've learned what the frogs say when they croak." The father grew angrier than ever, jumped up, and called all his servants, and said: "This dolt is no longer my son. I disown him. Take him out into the forest and kill him." They took him out into the forest, but when it came time to kill him they let him go.

The boy wandered from place to place. After a while he came to a castle and asked for a night's lodging. "Very well," said the lord of the castle. "If you are willing to spend the night in the old dungeon, you may stay, but I warn you, you will be facing great danger, for the place is full of wild dogs that bark and howl night and day. At certain hours a human must be brought in to them, and they devour him on the spot." The boy, however, was fearless. "Just give me some food for your barking dogs," he said, "and take me down to them. They won't hurt me." Since he himself insisted, they gave him food for the wild dogs and led him down into the dungeon. The next morning, to everyone's amazement, he came up safe and sound and said to the lord of the castle: "The dogs have told me in their language why they are living down there and bringing evil upon the country. They are under a spell and forced to guard a great treasure that is in the dungeon. They will know no peace until someone digs it up, and I have learned by listening to them how it can be done." All those who heard him were overjoyed, and the lord of the castle promised to adopt him as his son if he performed the task. Down he went again and brought up a chestful of gold, and from that time on the howling of the wild dogs was never heard again.

Some time later the boy, now a young count, took it into his head to go to Rome. On the way he rode past a marsh where some frogs were croaking. He pricked up his ears, and when he heard what they were saying he grew thoughtful and sad. At length, he arrived in Rome. The pope had just died, and the cardinals couldn't make up their minds whom to choose as his successor. In the end they agreed to wait until God sent a sign. Just as the young count entered the church, two snow-white doves flew down and perched on his shoulders. In this the cardinals saw a sign from heaven and asked him on the spot if he wanted to be pope. At first, he was undecided, for he didn't know if he was worthy, but at length he said, "Yes." Then he had to say Mass. He didn't know a single word of it, but the two doves, who were still perched on his shoulders, whispered it all into his ears.

The Three Languages
THE BROTHERS GRIMM

From kindergarten on, if not before, we are all told to pay attention. Although no one feels it necessary to explain what this means, we gradually learn that it means being still and focusing only on the matter at hand. Should our focus wander, we call it getting distracted.

As Grimms' tale suggests, however, when children or adults are distracted they are paying attention to something else. Whether it's soap falling into the bathtub, an apple falling from a tree, or the peculiar way an insect moves across the floor, small attractions may lead to bigger ideas. Being distracted, in short, means otherwise attracted.

Sometimes, however, we want to pay attention, but find it difficult, as when we have trouble becoming involved in a book. Many on-the-job accidents, from airline disasters to accounting mistakes, result when individuals are distracted from the task at hand. It may help to understand why such problems are widespread if we recognize that when we are distracted, we are attracted to something else. From this perspective very different questions come to mind: What is so attractive about the alternative stimulus? What can we learn from that attraction? Can we add the attractive elements to the stimuli to which we want to attend?

Sometimes we are stressed and want distraction. When thoughts about an impending divorce, an operation, or a move to a new city prove anxiety provoking, we often seek relief by trying to occupy our minds with other things. We may find temporary relief, but if the issue in question is important to us our minds find a way back. Rather than trying to think about something else, a more effective strategy may be to think about the problem differently. In research Irving Janis, John Wolfer, and I conducted we taught people about to undergo major surgery to reframe the hospital experience.[1] We asked the group to view the experience from a more adaptive perspective, to attempt to notice the advantages of being in the hospital. Having time to take stock of goals or to get in touch with family and friends who had been taken for granted or even a forced weight loss can be seen as an advantage. The potential advantages vary from person to person. Patients in this group felt less stress, took fewer pain relievers and sedatives, and left the hospital sooner than did patients who were not given this preparation. The desire to be distracted was the desire to be otherwise attracted.

Labeling behavior as distracted may be presumptuous. What we call distraction may be a deliberate attending to something other than what we think is important. As we will see later, this distinction may be significant when trying to understand the pervasive problem of so-called attention-deficit disorders.

THE PUZZLE OF ATTENTION

Before deciding that we, or our children, have difficulty paying attention, it is interesting to think about the situations in which paying attention presents no problem. When we get dressed in the morning, look up a phone number, or play computer games, we are generally quite able to find the requisite attention. We check out our closets and think about the weather and the occasion. We are able to find our address books and stay cued in to the letters of the alphabet as we search for the desired phone number. Some of us can patiently, even excitedly, sit for hours and follow the on-screen instructions for computer games. Indeed, to accomplish virtually anything, we need a modicum of attention. Since we are so successful most of the day at paying attention, perhaps we should look more closely at those situations in which we find it difficult, rather than blame the problem on lack of character or a mental deficit.

Students who do poorly are told to pay attention, focus, or concentrate with the understanding that if only they did, they would learn the intended lesson. What "paying attention" actually means is not examined. We just assume that if we could fix our minds on the matter at hand and not let them wander, all would be well. Perhaps we see ourselves as photographers trying to bring an object into focus and hold both the camera and the target still. Is this what we mean when we try to pay attention? Do we try to immobilize our minds and focus on a single subject?

We asked several high school teachers what they meant when they asked their students to pay attention, focus, or concentrate on something. We asked whether they meant that the students should "hold the picture still" in their mind or did they mean that the students should "vary the picture" in their minds? Teachers overwhelmingly chose the first alternative. When we asked the students what their teachers meant when they said to pay attention, focus, or concentrate, the students gave the same answer. There does not seem to be a problem with communication. The problem appears to be elsewhere.

As early as 1898, William James noted that something attended to appears to change even as one attends to it. The example he used was the difficulty we face when trying to stare at a finger. Just look at your finger without shifting your eyes. It is hard to do this for very long. Try to focus on a painting. Don't let your eyes wander across it, just keep the image still. Focusing on an object in this way is difficult at best. Researchers of perception tell us that the image actually fades from view.[2]

I think the same problem occurs when trying rigidly to hold an idea in mind. The difficulty may be more apparent to those who meditate. When meditators repeat a mantra or attend to their breathing, for example, their minds may wander to other thoughts. Once they notice that they are thinking about something, rather than think more about the thought, they return to the mantra, until their minds pull to another thought, and the sequence continues. Although this routine serves the very useful function of teaching meditators how to let go of mundane thoughts that entrap them, it also illustrates how natural it is for the mind to seek variety.

For us to pay attention to something for any amount of time, the image must be varied. Thus, for students who have trouble paying attention the problem may be that they are following the wrong instructions. To pay constant, fixed attention to a thought or an image may be a kind of oxymoron. Yet this is the very way people try to attend to the external world of things or the internal world of ideas. I polled twenty-five Harvard undergraduates, asking what it was that they did when they tried to pay attention. Twenty-one of them gave mindless strategies such as "Look at the professor"; "Write whatever is said." The others had slightly more mindful strategies but still with some residual attempt to fix attention.

People naturally seek novelty in play and have no difficulty paying attention in those situations. When something is novel we notice different things about it. If we see a stimulus as novel, for example, if we see a rosebush along a railroad track, we sit up and take notice. If we were to stare at the rosebush long enough, eventually we would become habituated to it. This pattern begins when we are infants and continues throughout our lifetimes. Changes in context or perspective lead us to notice novelty. If I am dating someone new who happens to be an architect, for example, I might attend to buildings that I pass every day but never really noticed. Noticing interesting things about the buildings would not be a strain. Successful concentration occurs naturally when the target of our attention varies.

The idea that to pay attention means to act like a motionless camera is so ingrained in us that when we do pay attention successfully we are usually unintentionally changing the context or finding novel features in our subject. The research described next, which Todd Bodner and I recently completed, supports this conclusion.[3]

ENHANCING NOVELTY

We recruited a group of undergraduate students to work at a computer. The program displayed a color object on the screen for about twenty-two seconds. The task was to press a button as soon as the object disappeared from the screen. The computer recorded the reaction times, and displayed another object two seconds after the button was pressed. The objects were either familiar shapes, unfamiliar shapes of several different colors, or objects of a single color.

We varied the instructions we gave to the students concerning how to attend to the stimulus on the screen. One group, the pay attention group, was simply told to focus on and to pay attention to each stimulus on the screen and to hit the button as soon as it disappeared. Another group was instructed to trace the outline of the target on the screen and to press the button the moment it disappeared. The last group was told to think of the shapes in different ways and to notice different things about each shape. These students were also told to hit the key the moment the shape disappeared from the screen.

First, we measured the students' memories for the figures seen on the screen. Clearly, we are more likely to remember something if we attend to it than if we do not attend to it. One could argue that memory is the most meaningful measure of attention. We also measured the students' views of the difficulty of the task. The group asked to think of the shapes in different ways, the mindful group, outperformed the other two groups in remembering color and shape. The shape and color scores for each subject were combined to create an index of overall stimulus memory. The mindful attention group significantly outperformed both the pay attention group and the tracing group. In comparison with the other groups, the mindful attention group also reported that the task required less effort and attention and was less frustrating. The tracing group and the pay attention group did not differ appreciably in their assessments.

In a further investigation, Martha Bayliss and I asked adults traveling by train to read short stories.[4] The mindful groups were instructed to vary either three or six aspects of each story: to read the text from different perspectives, to consider different endings, and the like. The focus groups were asked to focus on either three or six specific aspects of each story; that is, they were not encouraged to do anything more than take the information in as it was given in the story. A control group read the stories without any specific instructions. All the participants were told that they would be asked questions about each story after they finished reading it.

Participants were then asked to list all they could remember from the story they had just read. The people who had been asked to vary what they read, those in the mindfulness groups, remembered significantly more details than did members of the other groups. Those asked to consider six aspects of the story remembered more of it than did those asked to consider three. An interesting additional result was that the more novel the story, the less difference there was among the different groups.

Although the mindful groups had more to think about, they remembered more. Varying the target of our attention, whether a visual object or an idea, apparently improves our memory of it.

There are several ways to increase variability. As educators, we can present novel stimuli to our students. We can introduce material through games, because in games players vary their responses to fool their opponents or look more closely at all aspects of the situation to figure out how to win. Another approach is not to vary the stimulus, but to vary our perspective in relation to the stimulus. This situation happens often in physical play; in tennis or table tennis or any sport, we move around so that the stimulus is never quite the same. Perhaps bringing about a change in perspective through movement is how so-called hyperactive children increase novelty for themselves.

The most effective way to increase our ability to pay attention is to look for the novelty within the stimulus situation, whether it is a story, a map, or a painting. This is the most useful lesson to teach our children, because it enables them to be relatively independent of other people and of their physical environment. If novelty (and interest) is in the mind of the attender, it doesn't matter that a teacher presents the same old thing or tells us to sit still and concentrate in a fixed manner.

SOFT VIGILANCE

Not only is it nearly impossible to maintain attention by holding an image still, but it is also extremely fatiguing. (When people don't like doing something, it is often worth looking to see if they have a good reason.)

In psychological circles or when danger is involved, attention is often called vigilance. Staying vigilant is a big issue for pilots. Vigilance is considered effortful and seen to decline over time. In contrast, attention to the things we enjoy may be energizing and possible to sustain for long periods of time.

When horseback riding through the woods I used to be vigilant with regard to branches of trees extending beyond where they were supposed to be. My body would be tense as I tried to stay aware of the potential danger. It was tiring for both me and my horse. As I learned to become a more confident rider I was able to enjoy the surroundings, including the trees, and in so doing was also aware of any branches out of place. The advantage of this more varied attention was more than increased greater enjoyment; now I was open to noticing other potential hazards. Focusing hypervigilantly on tree branches made me vulnerable to other dangers on the trail. A kind of soft vigilance, or mindful attention, helped me "avert the dangers not yet arisen."

In contrast to hypervigilance, which locks in an object of attention, this soft vigilance remains open to novelty. With vigilance, the target of attention is static; with soft vigilance the mind, without detailed prescription, is open to take in more information.

RETHINKING ATTENTION DEFICIT HYPERACTIVITY DISORDER

Hypervigilance may be what we are unintentionally expecting from our students. As many as two million schoolchildren, along with their families, teachers, and classmates are affected by attention deficit hyperactivity disorder (ADHD).[5] Short attention span and easy distractibility, the cornerstones of this disorder, clearly have negative effects on scholastic achievement. Attention problems of this severity are not only evident in childhood, but often persist throughout life.[6]

The causes of ADHD are uncertain. Some theorists believe it has a genetic component, based on the relatively greater prevalence of ADHD in children whose parents exhibit similar symptoms. However, we would also expect to find this intergenerational similarity in the symptoms related to attention if parents taught their children to pay attention in the same way they did. Other studies suggest that children and adults with ADHD-related symptoms have less neurotransmitter activity in the areas of the brain thought to be important for the control of attention.[7] The data do not tell us whether there is less attention because there is less neurotransmitter activity, or whether there is less neurotransmitter activity because there is less attention, or both. Nevertheless, these data provide the rationale for the use of drug treatments for ADHD-related symptoms.

Stimulants, such as methylphenidate (Ritalin), are frequently used to treat the symptoms of ADHD, with some apparent success.[8] Although these stimulants may be effective in producing a quieter and less disruptive child, they do not necessarily help make a child a better student. In addition, the possible side effects, which include loss of appetite, decreased rate of growth, insomnia, stomach discomfort, irritability and mood swings, and development of tics, may further interfere with a child's ability to learn.

Nonpharmacological approaches are also used to manage ADHD. These include tutoring, usually in classes designed to help students with a variety of learning disabilities. Counseling is considered a vital part of the approach.

The prevailing conception of ADHD is that it is an illness. Treatment focuses on the symptoms that define the syndrome on the theory that if we treat the symptoms, school performance will improve. Treatment is left to the medical community, while educators assess the outcome.

By taking a new look at the nature of attention, educators might be able to improve school performance without medical intervention. A social psychological approach to ADHD would focus on the role of context and novelty in paying attention. The attention ability of ADHD children could be improved with changes in context, including changes in how information is presented and in environmental stimuli.

Steven Landau looked at the effects of distractions on the attention span of boys between the ages of six and twelve.[9] He looked at boys who were diagnosed as having ADHD and at boys without this diagnosis. They all watched several segments of educational television in the presence or absence of highly attractive toys. In the presence of the appealing "distractions," the ADHD boys spent only half the time spent by the non-ADHD boys watching television, but when the toys were absent the ADHD boys were able to pay attention to television.

Mary Ford found that attention increased when third and fourth graders diagnosed as having ADHD were working with computer software that used a game format.[10] Frances Cripe found that children with ADHD demonstrated decreased activity and increased attention when listening to rock music as they performed their task.[11] And Sydney Zentall found that when the stimuli were in color, attention increased.[12]

Some of the problems associated with treating ADHD and other attention problems may result from a lack of appreciation of the importance of novelty. Hyperactivity may be the child's implicit effort to increase novelty. If so, the advice to sit still and pay attention may be counterproductive.

Graduate students Shelley Carson and Margaret Shih and I[13] tested this movement and mindfulness hypothesis with a "normal" population of grade-school students aged nine to twelve who attended a traditional private school in Massachusetts.

The children were shown a poster of a character walking along a path. Fourteen landmarks, such as the Leaning Tower of Pisa, the Eiffel Tower, and the Pyramids, were pictured. The task was to pay attention to the poster and to try to remember the landmarks and where on the poster they were located.

Children in the mindful movement group were told to move slowly back and forth between two lines of masking tape set about seven feet apart on the floor while they were looking at the poster. We assumed that such movement would vary the perspective from which they viewed the poster. They were given a few minutes to practice until they felt comfortable doing the movement.

Children in the no-movement group sat still as they viewed the poster and were given a few minutes to get comfortable in their chairs. To make sure that any difference between these two groups would be the result of the change in perspective and not of a difference in physiological arousal, we added another control group. Children in this group sat in their chairs and shuffled their feet while they looked at the poster. Pretesting revealed similar heart rates for the two movement groups.

After the children viewed the poster they were given cutouts of landmarks that were on the poster as well as of landmarks that had not been seen before and they were asked to reconstruct the poster.

Children in the shuffling control group outperformed the sitting-still group. The movement group outperformed both groups and remembered significantly more landmarks. While conducting the experiment we noticed that children in the two control groups appeared to scan the poster in a linear fashion, resting their eyes on each landmark for a few seconds. In contrast, children in the mindful-movement group appeared to be viewing the poster as a whole and scanned it both vertically and horizontally.

To assess in another way whether novelty was in fact the reason for these results, we tried the experiment again with children from a Montessori school. At this school continuous movement was not only allowed but was even expected of children. We created the same three groups, but now our hypothesis was reversed: we expected the best memory performance to be in the now-novel sit-still group and the worst to be in the walking group. Our hypothesis was confirmed.

These studies suggest that mindfully varying perspective helps us pay attention. Margaret Shih, Amy Thau, and I are now testing the mindful learning hypothesis with children diagnosed as having ADHD. Being able to pay attention without walking around the stimulus or having to rely on somebody else to vary it for us has advantages. In our study children with ADHD are given instructions on how to vary the target of their attention in their own minds. To assess the effectiveness of these mindfulness instructions for children with ADHD we are using the same computer program that was used with college undergraduates in the study described earlier. Although it is too soon in this research effort to be certain of the findings, pilot data look encouraging; giving instructions to vary the target of attention seems to lead to an improvement in the ability to pay attention to a subject and remember what was learned.

In summary, our understanding of problems of attention may itself benefit from a shift in perspective. It is useful to begin by remembering that those of us who have problems paying attention can and do successfully attend to many things in the course of a day when we are not self-consciously "paying attention." Next, we can reframe the concept of distraction by conceiving of it as being otherwise-attracted. Finally, it is important to note that trying to hold an image or an idea still is difficult and unnatural. These observations suggest the importance of novelty to the process of paying attention. Whether trying to improve the ability to pay attention of college undergraduates, of children, or of children diagnosed with ADHD, we have found in our studies that instructions on how to seek out novelty, and thus pay mindful attention, appear to enhance performance.

3

The Myth of Delayed Gratification

My initial experiences of formal education were on the whole pleasurable. Reading and writing caused me no suffering. I found the first easier, but the second was enjoyable—I mean artistically enjoyable—and came to admire my own handwriting in pencil, when I got to that stage, perhaps as a youthful Chinese student might admire his own brush strokes. It was wonderful to see that the letters each had different expressions, and that the same letter had different expressions at different times. Sometimes the two capitals of my name looked miserable, slumped down and sulky, but at others they turned fat and cheerful, almost with roses in their cheeks. I also had the "First Grade" to look forward to as well as geography, the maps, and longer and much better stories.

The Collected Prose
ELIZABETH BISHOP

Our school years and later careers are permeated by such injunctions and beliefs as "If you work hard now, rewards will follow later" and "Once you do your homework, *then* you can go out and play." The retirement years are the "golden years." The consequences of this presumption for learning at any age have not been fully explored.

ALL WORK AND NO PLAY

When we think about work we often assume pressure, deadlines, the possibility of failure, fatigue, lack of choice, set goals, and unavoidable drudgery. We see play as the other side of the coin: energizing rather than enervating, freely undertaken for fun rather than outcome, relaxing rather than pressured.

Implicit in the concept of delayed gratification is the idea that work activities are necessarily arduous. If they were not, why would we have to be paid, or coaxed, or promised rewards to do them? This is not to deny that some people enjoy their work, but rather to understand what makes them different from those who don't.

> But yield who will to their separation
> My object in living is to unite
> My avocation and my vocation
> As my two eyes make one in sight.
> Only where love and need are one,

And the work is play for mortal stakes
Is the deed ever really done
For Heaven and the future's sakes.

Two Tramps in Mud Time
ROBERT FROST

Work and study are often seen as so unpleasant that we try to put them off as long as possible. Many of us would never complete tasks if not for deadlines. It takes time to get our minds working on these tasks even after we've sat down to do them. When we play tennis, cards, or tag, on the other hand, we launch directly into the fray. We don't first have to overcome mindsets about drudgery or fear of failure and work ourselves up to these activities, we simply play.

Delaying enjoyment makes sense if there are things that must be done *and* there is no evident way to enjoy doing them: Medical school is a killer, but that's what you have to do if you want to practice medicine; doing the laundry is boring, but it's necessary if you want the kids to have clean clothes; if you're good now, you'll be rewarded in the hereafter. Is it true, though, that medical school, laundry, or being good have to feel like work? They do not feel this way for everybody.

Learning anatomy by memorizing all the parts of the body is tedious; but what if it were a board game or a jigsaw puzzle in which we got to assemble or disassemble people we knew? Or consider the cliché that students of medicine think they have virtually every disease they study. Once you really think you have a disease, learning its symptoms, etiology, and cure may still not be fun, but it certainly isn't as hard.

My colleague Roger Brown points out that the work that we do in order to gain future rewards often turns out to be absorbing and a pleasure, whereas the rewards, when they arrive, may seem unimportant: "Writing, studying data, et cetera turn out in retrospect to be our greatest, most reliable pleasures, rather than the little trinkets of achievement (awards, et cetera) for the sake of which the work was supposedly undertaken."

Rewards found in the present are certain. Delayed rewards may feel empty ("To think of all I gave up for *this* . . ."). To justify waiting, the future must promise a bigger payoff. Yet the promise of a big payoff diminishes our appreciation of the present situation. Doesn't waiting sometimes make the reward sweeter? Perhaps so, but taken to extremes, this may be an unhealthy trade-off, along the lines of knocking our heads against the wall because it feels so good when we stop. To be sure, the highs can be experienced only if there are lows. But the alternative to steep peaks and valleys is not a perpetual, flat emotional experience. Total involvement, when, as Frost put it, work becomes "play for mortal stakes," provides a steadier, fuller, ever-present gratification.

If we don't open the presents until Christmas, or if we plan a trip for after the new year, aren't we delaying gratification? We are not, if the anticipation itself is positive. Compare leaving on a trip the same day you decide to go with planning to leave in three weeks. You might spend the three weeks actively planning the trip, gathering information, imagining all the fun you will have. The trip might even turn out to benefit from such thoughts. This is hardly delaying gratification; it is merely being gratified by anticipation as well as by the actual trip.

There are two approaches that educators and parents typically use to encourage children to engage in a disliked activity, whether it is homework or household chores. They promise children that rewards (or punishments for noncompliance) will follow, or they add fun elements to the unpleasant task. In both cases they reinforce children's presumptions that the task is odious.

Children are plied with stories that encourage this attitude: sweeping ashes from the fireplace all day leads to an encounter with Prince Charming; taking care of frightening old hags with huge teeth leads to pots of gold; and grasshoppers who chirp and sing in the meadow all summer will starve, while the lowly ant toiling in the dusty granary will be praised and rewarded.

For children to learn that they should forgo immediate pleasures and invest time and energy in activities that will have greater payoffs in the future, they have to assume that the world is just and orderly and predictable, that is, that we all get what we deserve.[1] The belief in a just world offers further support for the idea of delayed gratification. (It also supports a tendency to blame the victim. If people are seen as getting what they deserve, it is a small step to believing that victims must have deserved what they got.)

TURNING PLAY INTO WORK

A writer friend of mine was trying to concentrate on writing when some school-age children started up a hilarious, noisy game below his window. He asked them to leave. Since he was breaking up what clearly seemed a delightful scene, he paid them each a quarter for doing so. The next day they came back and caused the same annoyance; again, he paid them to leave. This routine continued for over a week, until one day my friend found he was out of quarters, and he suffered through the racket as best he could. He discovered that he could work despite the disturbance, and thence he gave no more quarters. The children stopped coming. Two weeks later he ran into one of them at the market and asked why he and his friends no longer came around. The child replied, "What do you think, we're going to come for nothing?"

Rewarding behavior often has just this effect: overjustifying the behavior so that its intrinsic value is overlooked.[2] The children came at first because it was fun for them. After being paid, they kept coming for the reward. Even play can lose its intrinsic value if it is done with another goal in mind.

> Who first invented work, and bound the free
> And holiday-rejoicing spirit down?

> *Work*
> CHARLES LAMB

Who among us has not had the experience of some task, initially enjoyed, coming to feel like work? Beginning a garden is enjoyable. Weeding it may not be. Trying a recipe for the first time may be totally engrossing. Preparing it again may not be. Shooting baskets is great fun. Competing may turn it into work. Repetition may be part of the problem. Adding other motives such as doing it because we have to, fear of evaluation, or letting the outcome overshadow the process can also turn play into work. For instance, cooking may be more fun for men than for women because typically, men are not expected to be good at it (or perhaps are not expected to do it at all).

Most tasks are not inherently pleasant or unpleasant, but an evaluation imposed on a task carries such a presumption. Virtually any activity can be made into work, and most, if not all, activities can be enjoyable. Solving math problems is unpleasant for many students, yet some of these same students buy magazines full of brainteasers. The fear of negative evaluation colors much of the school experience for most people. Claude Steele showed that black students often distance themselves from academic matters in order to protect their self-esteem.[3] In one study students were told that they would or would not be tested on the material they were given to learn. Black students performed perfectly well except when they believed they were being tested. Although the anticipation of being tested can affect us all, Steele contends that black students face additional anxiety about the possibility of confirming a negative academic stereotype. Such an effect can be understood in full measure when we remember how inextricably bound were our own school experiences and our anxiety about being evaluated.

To test the way we evaluate the pleasure of activities depending on the context or the label we put on them, Sophia Snow and I conducted a study.[4] We looked at whether people would regard the same activity differently depending on whether it was called work or play. Adults from the Boston area engaged in one of three tasks involving a calendar of Gary Larson cartoons. Because the cartoons are amusing, the tasks were expected to be fun. For the first task, participants were asked to sort the cartoons into odd- and even-numbered days, then by month, and then to add up the number of cartoons. The other tasks were both more difficult and more engaging. For the second task, participants were asked to change one or two words in a cartoon to alter its meaning completely. For the last task, people were asked to sort the cartoons into categories of their own choosing, for example, most versus least amusing, those with dogs in them, and so on. For half the participants, these activities were referred to as a game; for the other half, they were described as work.

After the participants completed each task, we asked them how much they enjoyed it and how often their minds wandered while they were working on it. Subjects enjoyed doing the first task whether we called it work or play, but significantly more in the "work" group reported that their minds wandered while they were doing the task. For the two more difficult tasks, more participants enjoyed the tasks when they were presented as play than when they were presented as work. Once again, minds wandered twice as often in the "work" as in the "play" groups.

TURNING WORK INTO PLAY

For those who enjoy doing crossword puzzles, consider the fun in trying to come up with a word that fits the puzzle's requirements. Then imagine doing the same puzzle with the expectation of being graded on speed and accuracy. If we assume an activity is play, we approach it nonevaluatively and proceed to get involved in it. What makes the activity enjoyable is the process of going from not knowing to knowing. If there are several possible solutions and we narrow it down to one that works, the puzzle is more fun than if we only come up with one solution.

When we are involved, much of the pleasure resides in drawing distinctions or noticing things that, by the fact that we select them for noticing, are interesting to us. The Provincetown Art Association has an auction every year. I look over the paintings and plan to bid on one or two. I notice all the particulars about them: color, theme, style, and so on. I continue to draw distinctions and even try to imagine them in various locations in my house. The more I notice, the more excited I get about the potential purchase. Often at the auction I am outbid—by someone who has more money than I or someone who has gotten even more involved in the process. Whether I take home the painting or the money I went with, the activity is great fun, and year after year I wait for the event.

In a work task, there tends to be little freedom as to the distinctions we attend to, or at least it appears so at first. Much of the work we do has rigidly prescribed steps: go over these twelve points when teaching the lesson; spell out these five features to the customer; set up the display in this way and in this order. But no matter how much in our work is spelled out, there is always room for finer choices and distinctions and for variations in our approach.

For students learning a history lesson, there seems little freedom in what they must study. Those are the facts that happened, and their task is to learn them. History was always my least favorite subject. I memorized all I needed to, but the task was always draining. It was as if I took Mark Twain's advice in *The Adventures of Huckleberry Finn* literally:

Persons attempting to find a motive in this narrative will be prosecuted; persons attempting to find a moral in it will be banished; persons attempting to find a plot in it will be shot.

BY ORDER OF THE AUTHOR

With all these possibilities forbidden or, more precisely, never taught, I never understood that involving myself in history by making idiosyncratic distinctions would make it fun to read. The only lessons I really learned were that history was about the past, not the present or future, and that it was not much fun.

We sort the activities in our lives into categories of work and play. These categories vary from culture to culture. The anthropologist Robert LeVine told me of field observations he made in a rural community in Kathmandu.[5] There, hight-caste Hindu men—fathers, grandfathers, teenage brothers, and uncles—take over the care of children for hours, not only when they feel like playing with them. They feed and wash the babies with evident enjoyment and affection. This activity does not seem to jeopardize their masculinity. Since the Nepalese Hindus are patriarchal, this was a surprise. High-status Nepalese prefer infant care to other tasks. Those who have been to school cut better deals so they can remain with the babies rather than go out in the field. Care of babies is seen as a leisure-time activity.

Among the Gusii of Kenya, in contrast, caring for a baby is considered menial work and carries a lower status. Men and teenage girls don't do it.

Virtually any task can be made pleasurable if we approach it with a different attitude. If we have long held a mindset that a particular activity is arduous, changing to a mindful attitude may be difficult, but the difficulty stems from the mindset and not the activity.

Stanley Milgram took advantage of the power of this approach when he ran some of his social psychology experiments in New York City. Most researchers pay people to encourage them to be subjects in studies, that is, they pay in return for work. Milgram on occasion had research assistants stand outside the Graduate Center of the City University of

New York carrying signs announcing that today, people could be in his research for free. He had many takers.

Lori Pietrasz and I tested the idea that even disliked tasks can be made pleasurable.[6] Participants in our study listened to or watched something for which they had no particular liking: either music tapes or televised football. For them this was much more a chore than a delight.

Participants who did not particularly like rap music heard a tape of rap music; those who had no liking for classical music heard a tape of classical music; and those who thought watching football was boring watched the Super Bowl. Participants were asked to notice three or six novel aspects about the activity. In each case, a control group was exposed to the same music or football game without instructions to make such distinctions. The groups instructed to draw distinctions chose their own. For football, it may have been particulars about the looks of the players or the interaction among teammates. For music, it may have been which instruments they could pick out or the meaning or lack of meaning of the words. In each case, we assessed people's liking for the activity before and after they became engaged in the task. Each group asked to draw distinctions ended up liking the activity more than before. The more distinctions drawn, the more the subjects liked the activity. There were no changes in liking for the control groups.

In another experiment, conducted with Andrea Marcus, participants were exposed to unfamiliar works of art.[7] All participants were shown two paintings. For the first, they were either instructed to notice novel aspects of the work or given no instruction about it. For the second, they were asked to make a comparative judgment. Rather than ask how much they liked the art, we wanted to see how deeply the involvement affected them. After the subjects viewed the art, we gave them a sheet of paper containing the titles of the two paintings. Under one title were several signatures; under the other there was only one signature. We asked participants to write their names under the title of the work they preferred. We wondered whether those subjects who mindfully approached the painting feel strongly enough about their preferences to go against the judgment purportedly made by the vast majority of other participants and select the unpopular work as their choice.

The people who drew novel distinctions were indeed less likely to conform. These participants were more confident of their feelings than were the subjects who had been asked merely to judge the paintings.

Social psychology includes a body of work on what is called the mere exposure effect. In the original study on this phenomenon, subjects were exposed to unfamiliar Turkish words.[8] The target words appeared on a list either several times or only once. Subjects were asked to make up definitions for these unknown words. Their definitions were then evaluated and rated according to how positive they were. Words that had appeared several times were defined in more positive ways.

Increased exposure to unfamiliar stimuli often has the effect of increasing liking. Liking seems to increase more for complex stimuli than for simple ones; more for exposure sequences that are varied than for those that are static; more for briefly presented words that are unrecognizable than for words that are recognizable; and in general more for people who have a greater tolerance for ambiguity.[9] Furthermore, boredom seems to limit the mere exposure effect.[10] These findings, taken together with the other studies described here, suggest that the mechanism behind this effect may be increased involvement, or mindful engagement as a result of exposure.

Mindful engagement not only increases liking for words and objects, but it also increases liking for people. Benzion Chanowitz, Richard Bashner, and I[11] showed slides of people with disabilities to children in elementary school and asked the children several questions about each person they saw.[10] The children were asked for one answer or for several answers to each question. For example, the children were shown a slide of a woman they were told was deaf. The control group was asked to name one way she might be good at her job as a cook and one way she might be bad at it. The other group was asked to name four ways she might be good at her job and four ways she might be bad at it. Next, the children were told that a child with a disability was coming to their school. They were asked if they wanted to attend a picnic with that child or have that child as a partner for various activities. Children who had been asked to provide a variety of answers in the earlier activity were less likely to want to avoid the new child, and their responses were more differentiated. For example, these children were more likely to want a blind child as a partner for an activity for which blindness could be an advantage, such as pin-the-tail-on-the-donkey, but not for an activity for which they thought blindness could be a disadvantage, such as a wheelchair race.

Drawing distinctions can have advantages other than making an activity fun. Many people making career plans are taught, implicitly or explicitly, to wait for something out there to grab them, to take hold of their interest. Year after year students are lost or unhappy because they don't know what career to pursue, as if without any involvement, they should know. Internships provide some information, but choosing an internship poses the same problem as choosing a career. We give up too much control if we wait to find careers that grab us. Involvement requires us actively to draw distinctions. Doing so often means breaking the activity into smaller pieces. Activities other than jobs—hobbies and pastimes— become enjoyable only with involvement. How many times have we seen people dragged around museums by a friend or spouse who's interested in what's there, when their own interest hasn't been piqued. Whether we are talking about art, a hobby, or the choice of a profession, more often than not people expect to know whether they'll like it before they engage in it. Clearly, many more choices open up to us when we realize that we can take a more active role in determining our preferences. If we don't take this active role, then even play can feel like work.

Pleasure is the state of being
brought about by what you
learn.
Learning is the process of
entering into the experience of this
kind of pleasure.
No pleasure, no learning.
No learning, no pleasure.

Song of Joy
WANG KEN

4

1066 What? or The Hazards of Rote Memory

. . . When the full moon had risen, Hansel took his little sister by the hand and followed the pebbles that glittered like newly minted silver coins and showed them the way. When they arrived home their father was delighted because he had been deeply troubled by the way he had abandoned them in the forest.

Not long after that the entire country was once again ravaged by famine, and one night the children heard their mother talking to their father in bed. "Everything's been eaten up again. We have only half a loaf of bread, but after that's gone, that will be the end of our food. The children must leave. This time we'll take them even farther into the forest so they won't find their way back home."

When their parents had fallen asleep, Hansel got up, intending to go out and gather pebbles as he had done the time before, but their mother had locked the door, and Hansel could not get out.

Early the next morning the mother came and got the children out of bed. They each received little pieces of bread, but they were smaller than the last time. On the way into the forest Hansel crumbled the bread in his pocket and stopped as often as he could to throw the crumbs on the ground. Little by little he managed to scatter all the bread crumbs on the path. The woman led the children even deeper into the forest until they came to a spot they had never in their lives seen before. "Just keep sitting here, children. If you get tired, you can sleep a little. We're going into the forest to chop wood, and in the evening, when we're done, we'll come and get you."

Then they fell asleep, and evening passed, but no one came for the poor children. Only when it was pitch black did they finally wake up, and Hansel comforted his little sister by saying, "Just wait until the moon has risen, Gretel. Then we'll see the little bread crumbs that I scattered. They'll show us the way back home."

When the moon rose, they set out but could not find the crumbs, because the many thousands of birds that fly about in the forest and fields had devoured them.

They walked the entire night and all the next day as well, from morning till night, but they did not get out of the forest. Eventually they became so tired that their legs would no longer carry them, and they lay down beneath a tree and fell asleep.

Hansel and Gretel
THE BROTHERS GRIMM

Hansel and Gretel lost sight of the bigger picture. Following bread crumbs on the implicit theory that following pebbles worked may seem easier than trying to memorize the forest, but neither strategy offers much control in new circumstances. Had they actively drawn distinctions and noticed finer points in their surroundings, as we will see, they might have had an easier time getting home.

Students who rely on rote learning may find themselves similarly helpless. Although the student who dutifully recites the multiplication tables or the Gettysburg Address may seem to be a figure from the past, most learning, especially preparation for tests, is still done by rote. "I know that material so well," an A student exclaims, "I could take that exam in my sleep." Most students still prepare by memorizing as many facts as they can from required reading and class notes. And many, if not most, teachers insist that students know key information as well as they know the backs of their hands.

LOCKING UP INFORMATION

Memorizing is a strategy for taking in material that has no personal meaning. Students able to do it succeed in passing most tests on the material, but when they want to make use of that material in some new context they have a problem. This disadvantage of rote memory applies to all of us, whether we are memorizing textbook information for school, technical information for work, or any other information.

I remember studying for a test as an undergraduate, memorizing the essential parts of an article by "Rock and Harris," and getting the question correct on the test. Later that same week when asked if I had ever read any of Harris's work, I said no. Had I been asked if I knew the work of "Rock and Harris" I probably would have replied yes. I learned the names as a package, and that was the way they stayed in my mind. A typical package, at least for those of my generation, is "Battle of Hastings/1066." I have no idea what to do with that fact, except when someone at a faculty meeting asks for examples of useless information that we all have at our disposal! If someone else says, "the Battle of Hastings," I always blurt out, "1066," still expecting to get my A. Interestingly, there is no one event that constitutes "The Battle of Hastings." Historians have given one name to a collection of events, each of which could be seen from a collection of perspectives, as is true for most of what we take as "facts."

We can watch a quiz show and answer many questions correctly (or else the show would not make satisfying televiewing), yet not have access to that information in any other context. For many of us, "William the Conquerer" exists only as the answer to the question, "Who fought the Battle of Hastings?"

Education traditionally has given students packages of information that are largely context free. Even when context is provided, the manner in which the information is presented still encourages mindless processing. Saying, for instance, that there were three reasons for the Civil War omits both context and perspective. What did a fifty-year-old Southern white man think the reasons were? A fifty-year-old black? A young Northern woman? And so on. When omitting points of view, the text or the teacher treats the information as true irrespective of perspective, that is, as a fact. Even if information is given from two perspectives, if the possibility of additional views is not intentionally built in, the tendency of students is to consider these two just as rigidly; there would simply be twice as much absolute information to memorize.

Most of us see memorizing as effortful and feel that learning too many facts can overload or clutter our minds. One middle-aged woman faced with remembering nine-digit zip codes and streams of digits in long-distance dialing, was overheard telling a friend that she was going to "give up state capitals" to make room.

Closed packages of information are taken as facts. Facts are taken as absolute truths to be learned as is, to be memorized, leaving little reason to think about them. Without any reason to open up the package, there is little chance that the information will lead to any conceptual insights or even be rethought in a new context. We can think of such encapsulated information as overlearned.

The disadvantages of rote memory have been pointed out over the years.[1] Higher levels of student boredom occur in schools that emphasize memorization and drills.[2] Some teachers try to provide opportunities for the development of knowledge through flexible understanding of course material. In math, teaching for understanding involves teaching students to think about what a problem means and to look for multiple solutions.[3] Studies have confirmed that science is better taught through hands-on research and discovery than through memorization alone.[4] In English, teaching for understanding means emphasizing the process of writing and exploring literature rather than memorizing grammar rules and doing drills.[5] Understanding is encouraged in history by turning students into junior historians.[6] These methods, all more effective than having students memorize material, are usually used sparingly and primarily with higher-level students even though virtually all students seem to be able to learn without memorizing.[7] Too many students still suffer the hidden costs of learning in the more familiar manner.

How often do children, or adults, for that matter, intentionally study the words of a song on the radio? Yet we often sing along after hearing a song only a few times. The learning took place without memorizing, without difficulty, and without fear of evaluation; most important, it was intrinsically motivating and fun.

How many bones of the body can we name even a week after our last biology class? Memorization appears to be inefficient for long-term retention of information, and it is usually undertaken for purposes of evaluation by others. It is difficult and rarely fun, although some of us may have enjoyed it because we were rewarded for having done it well.

We need only appeal to our own experience to be persuaded that material we once memorized is not readily available for use—either creative use or even use in the form in which we originally learned it. The same experience tells us that, except for certain individuals, memorizing is difficult. If it weren't, more students would do better on their exams. As students, we memorized material because we were instructed to do so. Memorization remains widespread for various reasons: teachers can easily grade academic performance based on memorized material; people believe that certain things (the basics) must be thoroughly learned before other areas can be tackled; the notion that there are basic truths in the world that are accepted by everyone creates a sense of stability; and, teachers are teaching in the same way they were taught—through memorization.

KEEPING INFORMATION AVAILABLE

There are alternatives to memorization: mindful ways to learn information so that it serves both the purpose of passing tests in school and that of keeping the information available for future creative use. As mentioned previously, memorization is a way of taking in material when it is personally irrelevant. Making the information relevant can remove the necessity for memorization. Read the following list of words and then look away and see which of them you remember: generous, helpful, authoritative, rigid, dependent, serious, funny, tender, weak, smart. Apart from the words at the beginning and end of the list, which we tend to remember because of their placement, the words we recall effortlessly are likely to be the ones that speak to our self-image. Information that is about ourselves, about the parts of ourselves we really care about, is the easiest to learn.[8] For instance, Hazel Markus and her colleagues found that people who have incorporated stereotypical ideas about masculinity or femininity into their self-concepts have better memory for words reflective of this stereotype than do people for whom the stereotype is less important.[9] Similarly, imagine that you are trying to lose weight but love eating greasy hamburgers. If someone tells you that one of those tempting burgers contains 2000 calories, your entire day's ration, you are likely to remember that number without having to repeat it over and over again to yourself. Psychologists call this the self-reference effect.

Many psychologists view the self as a complex, organized structure involving a variety of attributes or pieces of information about the person.[10] When information in a person's environment is relevant to any of these attributes it is more likely to be remembered. Steeplechase results are more likely to be remembered by those who are involved in horse racing, or who fancy themselves in that role, than by those who have no interest in horses.

The notion of relevance in education is hardly new, and just how relevant material should be has been hotly debated. One problem in making material relevant is the difficulty of doing so for several students at once—students from diverse backgrounds, with different interests and experiences.

There are two ways a teacher can make facts or ideas seem personally important. The most common approach is to shape or interpret ideas so that their relation to the lives, interests, and curiosities of the majority of students is readily apparent. When critics of education clamor for relevance, they are usually speaking of this sort of relevance. The second approach is to change students' attitudes toward the material, that is, to teach students to make the material meaningful to themselves.

This second approach is illustrated in the way in which actors learn scripts. They read a play through to get an idea of what it is about and to become engaged in its story and meaning. Before they attempt to learn their lines, they consider the meaning of the lines in relation to the larger plot and to the perspectives of the other characters. They begin to know what would bring the other characters to say what they say.[11] The illustration stops here, though, because at this point actors need to memorize the material. After all, each person's lines are cued by the exact lines that go before. Also, playwrights want to hear the lines they actually wrote, and directors expect control over what happens next.

DRAWING DISTINCTIONS

Noticing new things about any body of information is involving. When students draw distinctions, the distinctions are necessarily relevant to them. Distinctions reveal that the material is situated in a context and imply that other contexts may be considered. For instance, although few people worry about learning to watch sporting events, consider how seemingly irrelevant details in spectator sports can teach us about demographics or even prejudice. Suppose that a spectator notices that the majority of players on a certain team have blond hair. That person might wonder whether there is a relationship between hair color and that sport. This consideration could lead to noticing (caring about/being interested in) what hair color dominates among players in other sports. Such a seemingly trivial distinction could lead to an awareness of the absence of blacks or Asians or whites on some teams and to questions of what that absence might signify. As a more serious example, think about asking students to examine photographs taken of people at the time of the Civil War or the depression. Details observers note about expressions, clothing, and so on are the basis for much anthropological information about a period.

Drawing distinctions allows one to see more sides of an issue or subject, which is more likely to result in greater interest. Teaching students to draw distinctions sets the stage for mindful learning, that is, as noted in the introduction, for creating new categories, being open to new information, and being aware of different perspectives. Students learn to create working definitions that are continually revised and do not exhaust the potential phenomena. This kind of conditionally learned information is potentially accessible, even when not in the forefront of one's mind.

There is an analogy here in computer science. A computer that has virtual memory is one that swaps information to create the illusion of having more memory than it has; by swapping, a computer can appear to have much greater memory than its hardware permits. Computers achieve virtual memory by managing the activities run on them, so that at any one time only a fraction of the programs in use are under active consideration. Computers swap among applications so that current, but momentarily unused functions remain accessible (more so than when they are on a floppy disk in a drawer) without using up memory and the computer can effectively handle more information.

Recently Matt Lieberman and I examined the effects of a mindful attitude on the learning of reading selections.[12] We asked ninth-grade students to study one of two essays from their high school literature book: Sylvia Plath's "Reflections of a Seventeen-Year-Old-Girl," or O'Henry's "The Ransom of Red Chief." We asked half the students simply to learn the material. We expected that this instruction would result in students' trying to memorize the material. We asked the other students to make the material meaningful to themselves: "This may entail thinking about how certain parts of the information remind you of past, present, or future experiences, how the information could be important to yourself or someone else, or simply finding some significance of the story in relation to anyone and/or anything. Remember, what is meaningful to one person is not necessarily meaningful to another."

We then told half of each of these two groups that they would be tested after the reading period. We thought that the inclination to memorize would be so strong that the belief that a test would follow would cause even the group instructed to make the material relevant to memorize the material and thus make the learning less effective and less fun than if they had engaged with the material.

After a twenty-minute reading period, a test was given to all students. The test asked students to recall a number of facts from the story and to write a creative essay using the material in the story in their own way.

For homework, students were assigned another reading with the same instructions they received for the first. They were all tested again four days later.

The essays were judged by raters who were unaware of the groups' instructions. Students who learned the material in the traditional manner and were told of an impending test performed worse than all other groups. They tended to recall less information, and they showed less improvement from the first test to the second. The students instructed to make the material relevant, regardless of whether they expected to be tested, showed improvement in the intelligence and creativity of their essays.

Although we encouraged half of the subjects not to memorize the information, they did not necessarily follow our instructions. After each test we asked the students how they went about learning the material. Twelve of the twenty-eight students asked to make the material relevant nonetheless used only memorization to learn it. When we compared these students with the students who did follow the instruction, we found that the students who did not rely on memorization outperformed the others on every measure: they recalled more information from both readings; the essays they wrote were judged to be more creative and intelligent; and their scores improved from the first to the second test.

In a second experiment, Matt Lieberman and I tested this idea with tenth graders.[13] The students were assigned a chapter from a high school history book about the passage of the Kansas–Nebraska Act presented by Senator Stephen Douglas. To make the episode meaningful to them, students in one group were asked, in addition to reading from their own perspective, to read the passage from the perspective of the main character, asking what they would think or feel in his place, or from the perspective of his grandchild, asking what he or she might think or feel. We asked a control group simply to learn the passage. We tested all students at the end of the class period. One week later we surprised all the students with a second test on the chapter.

The group who read the material from more than one perspective, that is, mindfully, outperformed the control group on recall of the information, improvement from the first to the second test, creativity in the essays, and intelligence, or insight, of the essays. Again, essays were judged by outside raters.

Since memorizing is the standard approach students take to learning material, it is encouraging to see that after so many years of learning this way, so many of them are willing to learn the material in a new way. Students in our studies not only made the material meaningful to themselves, but they used different perspectives and thus were introduced to the context-dependent nature of information. Approaching information in this way invites further distinction drawing, further interpretation. Because the information is not all tied up in a nice, neat package, there is reason to get involved with it.

In other work, Claudia Mueller and I assessed memory as a function of conditional learning.[14] We showed ninth-to-twelfth-grade students pictures of ten ambiguous drawings (for example, one that could be described as a ball on the ground or a balloon tied to the middle of a stick). We presented the pictures either conditionally ("This could be . . .") or with absolute language ("This is . . .") and asked the students to remember them. Tests of recall and recognition of the objects in a new context revealed that conditional learning resulted in better memory.

For her thesis, Janet Eck tested the effects of memorization in a medical setting.[15] Because of the volume of information to be learned in medical school, medical students memorize more than do most of us. She hypothesized that when called on later to use that information in a somewhat novel context, students would overlook possible alternative views. She examined the diagnosis of diseases that were uncommon in women until recently. Since the vast majority of medical information has been deduced from the conditions in 150-to-170-pound white males, she wondered whether male doctors would be more likely than female doctors, who would be more familiar with the perspective of a female patient, to diagnose incorrectly a disease more common to men than to women. Male and female patients presented symptoms of medical ailments prevalent in women or prevalent in men. Male and female physicians were asked for their diagnoses. Not surprisingly, Eck found that the unusual syndromes, the ones not likely to have been memorized, went unnoticed and thus were misdiagnosed. In addition, women who presented signs of having had a transient ischemic attack or lung cancer were more likely to be misdiagnosed by male physicians than by female physicians, for whom the perspective was less unusual.

Information learned in an absolute form can be memorized. It remains still with each repetition, regardless of context and perspective. When we are told that something "could be," we understand immediately that it also could not be, or could be something else. When we teach important information, information about health, how to pilot an airplane, air-traffic control, bridge or building safety, and so on, we need to allow for exceptions, for information that goes beyond these common instances that appear to be all that is relevant at the time of initial learning. Students learning such information must be open to factors that could operate in a new context. If we simply memorize the known past, we are not preparing ourselves for the as-yet-to-be-known future.

Had Hansel and Gretel noticed more of their surroundings—how one tree differed from another, how the ground beneath them changed with the growth covering it, the odd rock or boulder strewn in the path—they would have had an easier journey home. In their case, as in many cases, memorization was impossible, but a mindful scan of the surroundings (in the forest, on the chessboard, at a party) will often help us navigate successfully.

5

A New Look at Forgetting

T*o forget is to let the grass*
overflow, and prefer
to the certain delight, the
uncertainty to come

Psalms
LUIS LLORENS TORRES

Especially as we age, we worry about forgetting much of what we have known. What would life be like if we remembered everything we once knew? Would I notice how you looked today if I kept before me clear pictures of how you looked every other time I saw you? Would I be inclined to listen to you if you said something at all similar to something else you once told me and I remembered every word you said? Would I taste the food I'm eating if I simultaneously remembered exactly how it tasted the last time? Wouldn't it be easier (more guilt free) to eat pasta, now considered healthy, if I did not remember that I was first taught that it was fattening? Would I even consider having another baby if the pain of every minute of the last delivery were still perfectly vivid?

A certain degree of memory is a necessary protection. We avoid touching hot stoves. A recollection that winters in New England can be cold is probably sufficient to lead one to buy a warm coat. To remember every sensation we felt when the temperature fell below zero and the winds reached sixty miles per hour, however, is probably unnecessary. There are clear advantages to forgetting bad experiences.

Is it ever good to forget good things? Forgetting pleasure allows us to re-experience it. We seek out others because of a general memory that company feels good. To be able to re-create the entire experience of a party might mean we needn't go to another. On first thought, that sounds like a good thing. We wouldn't need anybody or wouldn't need to make much effort because all we'd have to do is call up the memory. To do this, though, would mean that we were relying on pleasures enjoyed by younger, less experienced versions of ourselves. At what point would we want to freeze the experience? At twenty? Forty? Sixty? Would the experience be less rich and deep the earlier we froze it? My appreciation of novels, landscapes, and conversations is quite different for me now than it was when I was a teenager.

Continually re-experiencing life from a fresh vantage point is part of being truly alive.

STAYING IN THE PRESENT

It is easier to learn something the first time than it is to unlearn it and then learn it differently. The facts we are taught today often contradict what we were taught when we were much younger. Perhaps we would have a better feel for the nature of a quark if we hadn't been taught that electrons, protons, and neutrons were the smallest particles. Comprehending new complexities might be easier if we were not burdened by mindlessly memorized old information.

It is said that mathematicians do their best work when they are young. (The highest mathematics award, the Fields Medal, is given only to mathematicians under the age of forty.) Is this because they are not yet weighed down by too much knowledge, by mindsets they would be better off having forgotten?

Itiel Dror and I conducted three experiments to test the effect of knowledge on creative performance.[1] We explored whether a small amount of knowledge about a problem has a restricting effect on the ability to generate original ideas. Earlier research had established that certain kinds of previously learned information can restrict creativity.[2] That research examined creativity per se, that is, it examined originality as a goal in itself. In our experiments, we evaluated creativity as a means for accomplishing a desired goal, that is, we looked at the appropriateness and utilitarian value of the generated ideas.

In each experiment undergraduate participants were required to build a bridge over an imaginary river using small, custom-made wooden blocks. They were told that the height of the bridge would determine the size of the boats that could use the river, so the higher the better. Half the participants were briefly shown examples of how the blocks could be used in a different building task (building the longest bridge possible or building a tower). The other half had no prior exposure to the blocks. In the first experiment, 92 percent of the group that saw the examples used the blocks in formations identical to ones they had been shown, whereas only 8 percent of the group that did not see any examples used such formations. The prepared group came up with two solutions; the unprepared group came up with ten. We replicated these results in two other experiments. Our hypothesis in these experiments was that the group shown examples would have difficulty forgetting those examples. Our hypothesis was confirmed.

In social psychology there is a well-known phenomenon called the sleeper effect. People hear persuasive arguments by sources that are either credible or not and are later tested to see whether their attitudes have been affected by the communications. Initially, source credibility seems to matter. If the source of the message is someone we respect, we are more likely to be influenced than if we view the source of the message as untrustworthy. The interesting aspect of the phenomenon, however, is that over time, the credibility of the source ceases to matter. People forget where they heard it or from whom, but they retain general aspects of the persuasive message. This effect seems to support the belief that any publicity is good publicity.

Related work in social psychology has shown that over time people are more likely to make dispositional than situational attributions.[3] That is, people are more likely to consider several aspects of the situation in their explanations when they try to explain behavior soon after it has occurred than when they try to explain it later. As they forget the details of the situation, the explanation becomes more global. For example, "He was late because of the weather" may be replaced with the attribution, "He is inconsiderate."

When people forget details, they often supply their own in ways that fit their particular interpretation of events. They work backward and construct possible scenarios in accordance with their remembered general impressions. Typically, the particulars are more likely to be forgotten than is the basic situation.[4]

THE DANGERS OF MINDLESS MEMORY

We can remember information in two ways: mindfully or mindlessly. In previous chapters we saw that mindful learning enables us to be sensitive to context and to notice the present. When we have learned information mindfully, we remain open to ways in which information may differ in various situations. This sort of memory may guide our current behavior, as we are primed to notice the subtle changes. When we have learned something mindlessly, however, either by accepting information unconditionally or by overlearning or memorizing it, we may be better off forgetting such context-free facts so that we are not bound by them.

My notes before a lecture are sparse to nonexistent. I fear that if I write out all that I plan to say, it will be hard not to rely on past thoughts when I give the lecture again. Without a script, I'm forced to reinvent the lecture instead of delivering a canned one. I remember the general points, but the particulars have to be rediscovered. Preparing in this manner makes it much more likely that I will deliver a lecture that reflects my current thinking and the present situation; I'm not tied to a rigid outline or to reading notes. Moreover, I find that I feel excited by the possibility of coming to a new insight.

When re-membering is an active process, when we have the general idea, but search for details and in a Sherlock Holmes fashion figure out what we need to know, we feel accomplished. When we remember something without any constructive work, when we merely call up information in exactly the same form in which we encoded it, there is less reason for feeling masterful. It is far more satisfying to master something than *to have* mastered it. True, getting a high grade on a test because we have given back to the teacher exactly what we memorized the night before may be rewarding if it works, but it is surely less rewarding than figuring out a problem in the present.

Remembered facts are likely to be considered true. Yet truth often changes depending on context and over time. Forgetting allows us to arrive at better solutions because the new solutions are based on more experience and take into consideration the present context.

ABSENTMINDED VERSUS OTHER MINDED

We become aware that we have forgotten something only at the point when we want to remember it. Has the forgetting benefited us up to that point? Think of a person walking into her house trying to remember something important or trying to solve a personal dilemma. Would this time be better spent mindlessly memorizing where she places her keys? Perhaps when we can't find our keys it is because we were thinking about more important matters when we put them down. If that were not the case, why would we forgive the geniuses among us for their absentmindedness. For them we presume it is really other mindedness that is occurring. Why should it be different for the rest of us? Geniuses or not, once we recognize that we have forgotten something we need, we become oriented to the present and reinvent or rediscover what we need to know. In this sense, forgetting provokes mindfulness. Memorizing keeps us in the past; forgetting forces us into the present.

Most often, if we've learned something mindfully we needn't worry about remembering it. The information is likely to be there when we need it. A friend told me of a conversation with her mother. When my friend couldn't remember her friend's last name, she asked her mother what Susan's last name was.

Her mother said, "Susan who?" to which she replied, "Susan Goldman."

DOES MEMORY DECLINE?

The people most plagued by a negative view of forgetting are the elderly. A majority of Americans believe that their memory will inevitably decline in old age.[5] We pick up this stereotype as young children, and it is passed on from generation to generation, often with undesirable consequences. Information that is mindlessly remembered may be better forgotten. Mindsets about failures, be they about *poor* memory or any negative expectations may unnecessarily limit us.

Those who have investigated memory in the elderly disagree about the inevitability of this decline. Some argue that the cognitive deterioration that accompanies aging is wired into the nervous system, that is, that it is biologically determined. Others argue that an expectation of memory decline creates the reality and that if the expectation could be changed, many aspects of memory decline could be reduced. Those who consider the decline inevitable have conducted research to document trends of memory decline.[6] Those who believe, as I do, that memory loss can be a self-fulfilling expectation have tested whether changes in environmental factors can improve memory function among the elderly.[7] Although the results of this latter research suggest that permanent memory loss does not inevitably take place as part of the natural biology of aging, it has not yet become the dominant view.

Such expectations about memory loss may be part of more general expectations about aging. A meta-analysis of studies that examined evaluations of old people, confirmed that Americans hold negative attitudes toward aging.[8] The expression of negative stereotypes of aging tended to increase in the studies in which the researchers asked the subjects to evaluate old people's physical attractiveness or mental competence, such as their tendency to forget, rather than their general personality traits.

Charles Perdue and Michael Gurtman conducted a study that confirmed these findings and demonstrated that such views probably influence the thinking of many Americans at a level below awareness.[9] Subjects were primed by the rapid flashing (i.e., below awareness) on the computer screen of the word *old* or *young* prior to the appearance of a trait name on the screen. After reading the trait, the subjects indicated whether the trait was positive or negative. All subjects were then given a list of negative and positive traits randomly matched with either the question, "Do you think this describes a young person?" or the question, "Do you think this describes an old person?" The subjects were much more likely to recall positive traits that were randomly matched with the question, "Do you think this describes a young person?" and negative traits that were randomly matched with the question, "Do you think this describes an old person?" More important, subjects made decisions more quickly about the positivity of traits following the subliminal flashing of the word *young* and about the negativity of traits following the flashing of the word *old*.

The mechanism by which these negative stereotypes about aging influence our thinking as we become old may be understood in terms of the effect called premature cognitive commitments.[10] These are mindsets that we accept unconditionally, without considering or being aware of alternative forms that the information can take. As mentioned before, once a person processes information unconditionally, these now-accepted facts do not come up for reconsideration.

Unconditional acceptance of information occurs frequently with information that initially seems irrelevant, such as information about old age that we encounter in childhood. A child may hear about a forgetful, cranky, old person and allow this image to become the foundation for everything learned about old age.[11]

The Old Man and His Grandson

There was once an old man who was almost blind and deaf and whose hands trembled. When he sat at the table, he could hardly hold his spoon; he liked to talk and he took forever to eat his supper. His son and his son's wife lost their patience and finally made the old man sit in a corner behind the stove. They brought his food in an earthenware bowl. He looked sadly in the direction of the table, and his eyes filled with tears. One day his hands trembled so much that he dropped his bowl and it fell to the floor and broke. The young woman scolded him, but he said nothing and only sighed. She bought him a wooden bowl for a few kreuzers, and from then on he had to eat out of it. As they were sitting there one day, the little four-year-old grandson was on the floor playing with some pieces of wood. "What are you doing?" his father asked. The child replied: "I'm making a trough for both of you to eat out of when I'm grown-up." Husband and wife looked at each other for a while and burst into tears. After that they brought the old grandfather back to the table. He ate with them from then on, chatted merrily and took his time.

ADAPTED FROM THE BROTHERS GRIMM

In this case, the father and mother had a chance to change their ways and the son learned that things could change. More often than not, however, such attitudes go quietly uncorrected.

ALTERNATIVE VIEWS OF MEMORY AND AGING

Becca Levy and I conducted research on memory and on attitudes toward aging in two cultures in which we believed negative stereotypes of aging were not as widespread or as widely accepted as they are in most of the United States.[12] Because of their independence from mainstream American culture and the frequent observation that these cultures hold their aged members in high esteem, we looked at mainland Chinese and the American Deaf.[13]

Our hypothesis was that if negative views contribute to memory loss in old age and our selected groups hold more positive views of aging than do non-hearing-impaired Americans, then both the Deaf and the Chinese people would show less memory loss with aging.

By selecting two cultures that share little besides their positive views toward aging and an independence from mainstream American culture, we tried to reduce the likelihood of what psychologists call cohort effects, that is, other experiences shared by members of the same age group that could account for any possible enhanced memory findings among the elders of these two cultures. In other words, if we looked only at American cultures (hearing and deaf) and found the predicted interaction, we would not know whether it was a result of the different cultural stereotypes about aging or of another confounding factor. For example, studies suggest that a stigmatized status can lead to the development of cognitive coping skills; thus the members of the old, Deaf cohort might have preserved their memory skills because when they grew up, there was more prejudice against Deaf people than there was when the younger cohort grew up.[14] Fortunately, the two Chinese age cohorts are not stigmatized. By studying diverse cultures we do not eliminate all possible cohort effects, but we reduce their likelihood.

The Chinese hearing and American Deaf cultures fit our research specifications. Although they differ in such areas as language, food, history, appearance, kin traditions, and societal demographics, both cultures tend to be intergenerational and to hold their elders in high esteem. An anthropological study of Deaf elderly living in San Francisco found that adults of all ages identified and interacted with one another at various social events, including at Deaf clubs which meet several times a week.[15] A similar phenomenon was found in east coast Deaf clubs.[16] Younger members of the Deaf community often treat older Deaf adults as role models and wise leaders.[17]

Chinese culture also has a long tradition of honoring the elderly. In the two thousand years preceding 1949, the practice of ancestor worship and the Confucian values of filial piety and respect for the old prevailed, endorsed by the government.[18] In 1949, when the Communist Party took over leadership of the state, official attitudes temporarily changed. The Communist leaders banned Confucianism, religious practice, and ancestor worship because they felt that these practices might threaten the expansion of state and party power.[19]

One might have expected this change of policy to harm the status of the elderly and the positive expectations about aging in China; however, the Chinese people still speak of advanced years with pride.[20] Even though the original Communist leaders did not expect the position of elders to remain strong, "the Communist Revolution has strengthened rather than weakened traditional views of old age."[21]

In the United States, from an early age deaf individuals are not exposed to the conversation that is the background of ordinary hearing life, in part because 90 percent of deaf people are born to hearing parents who usually do not communicate by sign language.[22] The deaf also cannot listen to the radio and until the implementation of recent technological advances were rarely able to understand the dialogue and narrative of television and movies. One advantage of such isolation may be reduced exposure to negative stereotypes about aging.

In the three cultures (mainland Chinese, American Deaf, and hearing American) we measured the following three hypotheses: (1) The Chinese and hearing-impaired American cultures hold more positive views of aging than does the hearing mainstream American culture. (2) Young subjects in each culture perform similarly on the memory tests, whereas the elder Chinese and American Deaf participants outperform the elder hearing American group. (3) There is a relationship between positive views toward aging and better memory performance found among the older subjects.

We selected thirty participants from each culture. Half the members of these three groups consisted of young adults (aged 15 to 30 years; mean = 22 years), and half consisted of elderly adults (aged 59 to 91 years; mean = 70 years). We selected fifty-nine years as the starting age for the old group because in China, most women retire by the age of fifty-five and most men retire at the age of sixty;[23] in addition, age fifty-nine is about when people in the hearing-impaired community begin to attend social events planned for older adults.[24] We matched subjects in the three cultures by years of education, socioeconomic status, and age.

In the United States, experimenters recruited all participants from the Boston area. We recruited the fifteen younger hearing individuals from youth organizations and the fifteen older hearing participants from a senior drop-in center. We recruited the fifteen younger Deaf individuals from a Deaf cultural organization and the fifteen Deaf elderly from a senior drop-in center. In China, interviewers recruited the thirty subjects from a pencil factory located in the western district of Beijing. The fifteen younger subjects were currently working at the pencil factory, and the fifteen older subjects returned to the factory once a month to collect their pension checks.

To test memory, we showed subjects photos of elderly individuals whom they were told they would one day meet. For the hearing sample, each photo was presented for five seconds, the experimenter read a passage about an activity involving the photographed person (e.g., swimming every day), and then the subject examined the photo again. In the hearing-impaired sample, the statement about the activity was signed. For the Chinese groups, the photos were of elderly Chinese. All subjects were then shown the photos and asked to give us the matched activity.

The three groups of young subjects performed similarly on the memory task, as we had predicted. The elder Deaf and elder Chinese participants clearly outperformed the elder hearing group. There was no difference in memory performance between the two Chinese age groups.

We also rated the views toward aging in these three cultures by having subjects in each group answer the question, "What are the first five words or descriptions that come to mind when thinking of somebody old?" Answers were evaluated for positivity by raters who were unaware of the culture or age of the subject. We found that these views correlated with the performance of the three groups, that is, negative views correlated with poorer performance in the older groups. These results support the view that cultural beliefs about aging play a role in determining the degree of memory loss that people experience in old age.

The rigid mindsets we hold about ourselves affect our performance. These mindsets, including our beliefs about old age, are often unwittingly accepted at a time when they may seem irrelevant to our current concerns. Children who do not care about school may accept negative assessments of their abilities. Later, when they come to care about the particular abilities in question, these assessments are already fixed in their minds. At that point the damage is done. The mindset does not get tested; it is treated as though it is necessarily true. This may be how we accept the so-called inevitable memory decline with age. If we are led to believe that we have poor memories or that we are poor students, these mindsets can become self-fulfilling prophecies.

The negative assumption about mental capacity in old age can be seen in many adult education courses. Although there is no reason to believe that information imparted to older people should differ from that taught in colleges, catalogs aimed at older adults are filled with far more narrow topics. They typically deal with retirement and health issues or with lightweight courses in appreciating art or music. The experience of younger people in college courses may be shortchanged by the absence of older adults. Older adults are more likely to have had experiences that tell us that the new facts being imparted are more true in some contexts than in others. Diversity provokes mindfulness. Their more extensive and varied experiences may reveal the meaningfulness of certain information that would otherwise appear irrelevant. Not only is education not wasted on the old but, without their participation, it may be wasted on the young.

6

Mindfulness and Intelligence

A man who lived on the northern frontier of China was skilled in interpreting events. One day, for no reason, his horse ran away to the nomads across the border. Everyone tried to console him, but his father said, "What makes you so sure this isn't a blessing?" Some months later his horse returned, bringing a splendid nomad stallion. Everyone congratulated him, but his father said, "What makes you so sure this isn't a disaster?" Their household was richer by a fine horse, which his son loved to ride. One day he fell and broke his hip. Everyone tried to console him, but his father said, "What makes you so sure this isn't a blessing?"

A year later the nomads came in force across the border, and every able-bodied man took his bow and went into battle. The Chinese frontiersmen lost nine of every ten men. Only because the son was lame did the father and son survive to take care of each other.

Truly, blessing turns to disaster, and disaster to blessing: the changes have no end, nor can the mystery be fathomed.

The Lost Horse
CHINESE FOLKTALE

The very notion of intelligence may be clouded by a myth: the belief that being intelligent means knowing what is out there. Many theories of intelligence assume that there is an absolute reality out there, and the more intelligent the person, the greater his or her awareness of this reality. Great intelligence, in this view, implies an optimal fit between individual and environment. An alternative view, which is at the base of mindfulness research, is that individuals may always define their relation to their environment in several ways, essentially creating the reality that is out there. What is out there is shaped by how we view it.

Despite the emphasis in current intelligence theory on several kinds of intelligence, there is still an assumption of an absolute, external reality revealed by greater or lesser degrees of these various sorts of intelligence. This assumption is of more than academic interest; it may have detrimental effects on self-perception, perception of others, personal control, and the educational process itself.

As we will see in this chapter, belief that one's perceptions must correspond to the environment and that the level of correspondence is a measure of intelligence stems from a nineteenth-century view but continues to be influential today. A theory of correspondence between cognitive faculties and environment can be found in a variety of concepts of intelligence, ranging from Charles Spearman's[1] "g," a general factor that describes the correlation among many cognitive abilities, to Howard Gardner's[2] multiple intelligences, which are any socially valued abilities. The assessment of each ability depends on an assumption of a certain reality; the intelligence in question corresponds to that reality. For instance, the currently popular notion of emotional intelligence implies that certain people have a keener sense than others of what other people are actually thinking and feeling.[3] Research that my colleagues and I have conducted has shown how this theory of correspondence can be intellectually, emotionally, and physically debilitating.

Before discussing the damaging effects of such a view, it may be helpful to look for its source by tracing the roots of intelligence theory back to the nineteenth century.

NINETEENTH-CENTURY THEORIES OF INTELLIGENCE

In 1854, Hermann von Helmholtz observed a curious phenomenon. When he looked with each eye on a different-colored square—a red square for one eye and a green square for the other, with a divider separating the two—he was able to bring only one square into focus at a time; also, his attention tended to drift from one color to the other.[4] His inability to control what part of his perceptual world came into focus and his failure to bring these two pieces—these small squares—of experience together in a unified visual field led Helmholtz to extensive speculation and empirical research about the ways in which we make sense of our environment.

Our inability to attend to both of Helmholtz's images simultaneously—a phenomenon that has been frequently replicated—raises this question: If only one image can be within our perceptual field at a time and we cannot directly perceive the relation between these images, why do we automatically form a conception of their relationship? There are two approaches to answering this question. For many theorists of intelligence, the question is primarily epistemological: "How can I *know* what relationships exist among the pieces of my experience if I do not perceive the relations directly?" From the point of view of mindfulness theory, this question is primarily an issue of personal control: "Is my way of perceiving the relationships among the pieces of my experience so *automatic* that it is beyond my control?" The deliberately ambiguous image in Figure 1 may make these questions more concrete.

When quickly scanning the right portion of this image (labeled "i") many viewers see an enclosed structure from a perspective that looks up from below. The perceptual cue that the view is from below is the line that runs from *a* to *b* but does not continue to *c;* one side of the figure appears to be obscured by another. After then scanning the left portion of the figure (labeled "ii") several times, many viewers find that the image appears to flip so that they see the form from above. Although some viewers are able to voluntarily flip the

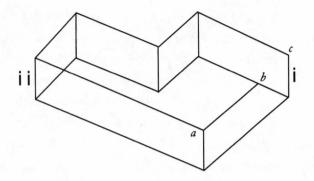

Figure 1   From J. Hochberg, "Attention, Organization, and Consciousness," in Attention: Contemporary Theory and Analysis, *ed. D. I. Mostofsky, p. 118 (New York: Appleton-Century-Crofts). Copyright 1970 by Meredith. Adapted by permission.*

perspective, most find that a perspective forms without their thinking about it.

We depend on this automatic organization of perception in almost every waking moment. This automatic structuring of experience generally serves us well by allowing us to interpret our environment almost effortlessly. The limits of this automatic organization can be seen in the experience with Figure 1. That many viewers, when focused on the left side (ii) of the form, are not oriented by the right side (i), indicates how limited our field of immediate perception can be. We often fail to keep these limits in mind. Regardless of our initial experience in viewing the figure, we are likely to agree that incorporating this figure into our experience requires no great cognitive leap. Most of us have a cognitive category, such as "optical illusion," that allows us to classify the figure and place it in the general conceptual framework through which we understand our world. However small this step from direct perception to a general conceptual framework may be, it is the first kernel of what we call intelligence.

The ability to place pieces of our experience in relation to one another was one of the criteria used by Sir Francis Galton, and later by Alfred Binet, to assess intelligence. In the nineteenth century Galton assessed intelligence by asking people to arrange a set of weights in order of heaviness, a test of sensory discrimination that was later adapted in the Binet–Simon Intelligence Test.[5] Galton also tested people's ability to bisect lines, a measure later used by James M. Cattell in some of the first intelligence tests administered in the United States. These early theorists believed that the basic capacity to organize perceptions was the basis of intelligence. Although Galton and Cattell's methods of testing perceptual skills were superseded by psychometric tests that focused on more complex cognitive tasks, their approach laid the foundation for the assessment of intelligence.

In the 1870s and 1880s, such theorists as Galton and Herbert Spencer, in addition to Charles Darwin, were applying evolutionary theory to human behavior.[6] The link between evolution and intelligence is important, not because of the endless, and perhaps fruitless, debate about the role of heredity in intelligence, but because the concept of evolution is necessary to understanding the organizing role that intelligence is believed to have on our perceptions.

Seen in an evolutionary framework, intelligence is an ability to retain and organize perceptions that enhance our chances for survival. The perspective we automatically impose on our perceptions is not merely an arbitrary construct, but an adaptive response determined by natural selection. The more closely our conceptual map corresponds to the contingencies of our environment, the greater our chances for survival.

In this view, the advantage more highly evolved animals hold over their less developed counterparts is the ability to take in ever more subtle perceptual cues and therefore create a more accurate cognitive map. This general trend toward increasingly fine discrimination, which Spencer[7] called the "principle of universal development," was outlined in 1909 by Edward L. Thorndike, the person perhaps most instrumental in bringing psychometric (intelligence) testing to the U.S. educational system.

> Our bodily descent is roughly as follows: fishes begat amphibia; amphibia begat reptiles; reptiles begat mammals; some early mammals begat the primates; some early primates begat man. . . . [T]he demonstrable intellectual difference between the year old baby and the monkeys is not that he has many ideas while they have few or none. He, too, has few or none. It is that he responds to more things and in more ways.[8]

This early conception of intelligence as a capacity for increasingly fine discrimination did not withstand the test of time. By the 1920s, psychologists had demonstrated that basic measures of perceptual discrimination could not be used to predict such skills as mathematical ability or ability in other academic areas, and mental testing began to focus less on general intelligence and more on specific abilities.

A mental ability is a probability that certain situations will evoke certain responses, that certain tasks can be achieved, that certain mental products can be produced by the possessor of the ability. It is defined by the situations, responses, products, and tasks, not by some inner essence.[9]

THE NOTION OF OPTIMUM FIT

By abandoning the idea of intelligence as increasingly fine discrimination and defining it instead as a relationship between specific situations and specific responses, theorists of intelligence paved the way for what we now call domain-specific intelligence.[10] Each domain has its own cognitive map, which an individual can use as a guide to operating effectively in that domain.

The most important task for future theorizing about intelligence is to specify better the interrelations between environmental context, on the one hand, and mental functioning, on the other.[11]

To understand this notion of optimum fit between individual and environment, let us try to apply it to our ambiguous Figure 1. Imagine that the figure is no longer a two-dimensional illusion, but a transparent, three-dimensional model designed to create a similar visual effect. This glass model is suspended about twenty yards away. The task is to throw a ball through its center. We must orient ourselves to this ambiguous form before tossing the ball through it.

Although such a task may appear fanciful and unrelated to what most of us think of as intelligence, the standard of optimum fit used by intelligence theorists presupposes that every pencil-and-paper measure of intelligence implies a real-life analogue. This imagined task is a specific case of the more general situation confronted by all living creatures: individuals must use their thinking skills to cope with the environment.

As we have seen, the right side (i) of Figure 1 provides the critical cue for accurate orientation. The fact that the line extending from *a* to *b* does not continue to *c* indicates that the correct orientation is a perspective looking up from below. Intelligent individuals will recognize this unambiguous cue (line *a-b*) and consequently form a mental image that accurately *corresponds* to reality. Having accurately conceptualized the figure, these people will have a better chance of tossing the ball through the suspended form than will those who have an inaccurate mental image of the figure.

An Alternative Ability

The concept of mindfulness, rather than referring to the ability of matching cognition to environment, shares with William James a skepticism of the very notion of correspondence.

Owing to the fact that all experience is a process, no point of view can ever be *the* last one. Every one is insufficient and off its balance, and responsible to later points of view than itself.[12]

In a mindful state, we implicitly recognize that no one perspective optimally explains a situation. Therefore, we do not seek to select the one response that corresponds to the situation, but we recognize that there is more than one perspective on the information given and we choose from among these.

The automatic processes involved in perception may well result from a long history of natural selection, and, when not determined by heredity, they probably are conditioned. Mindfulness theory, however, looks beyond these automatic perceptual processes to model higher-level thinking. In a mindful state, we take a second look at how our perceptions structure experience on the assumption that they are more malleable and susceptible to individual control than is apparent at first glance.

Returning to the ambiguous figure, recall that despite what appears to be an unambiguous cue at the right side of the figure (the line extending from *a* to *b* but not continuing to *c*), many viewers find that their perspective flips involuntarily. If we believe that the cues in the right half of the form are truly unambiguous, this slippery perception can be disconcerting. If, in order to feel in control, we must believe that we have a firm grasp on reality, the inability to hold this figure stable may be seen as a failure. Rather than following the implications of this

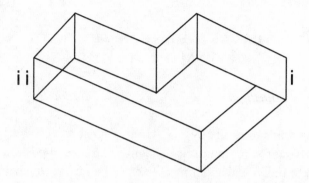

Figure 2   From J. Hochberg, "Attention, Organization, and Consciousness" in Attention: Contemporary Theory and Analysis, *ed. D. I. Mostofsky, p. 118 (New York: Appleton-Century-Crofts). Copyright 1970 by Meredith. Adapted by permission.*

unstable perception, we simply put the experience into a category called "optical illusion" and move on.

How would a viewer respond if the figure were three-dimensional? Imagine that the form now appears as shown in Figure 2. The contortions presented earlier as an impossibility, as two conflicting perspectives, now look perfectly reasonable. This form could be replicated as a three-dimensional object, as what we call a Möbius strip. After twisting one end of a strip of paper 180 degrees, Möbius glued the two ends of the paper together to create a form that twists back on itself so that it has only one side. By thinking of the form as three-dimensional, we gain a new perspective.

Table 1
DIFFERENCES BETWEEN INTELLIGENCE AND MINDFULNESS

Intelligence	*Mindfulness*
Corresponds to reality by identifying the optimum fit between individual and environment	Controls reality by identifying several possible perspectives from which any situation may be viewed
A linear process moving from problem to resolution as rapidly as possible	A process of stepping back from both perceived problems and perceived solutions to view situations as novel
A means of achieving desired outcomes	A process through which meaning is given to outcomes
Developed from an observing expert's perspective, which focuses on stable categories	Developed from an actor's ability to experience personal control by shifting perspectives
Depends on remembered facts and learned skills in contexts that are sometimes perceived as novel	Depends on the fluidity of knowledge and skills and recognizes both advantages and disadvantages in each

When we are mindful, we implicitly or explicitly (1) view a situation from several perspectives, (2) see information presented in the situation as novel, (3) attend to the context in which we are perceiving the information, and eventually (4) create new categories through which this information may be understood.

Some of the differences so far noted between mindfulness and intelligence are summarized in Table 1.

LINEAR VERSUS MINDFUL PROBLEM SOLVING

Contrast the example of the two figures with the kind of problem and problem-solving approach found in an educational setting. Intelligence theorists, working with a model of correspondence, view an ambiguous situation as a problem to be resolved.[13] Although such an approach may attempt to view the problem from several perspectives, the objective is to identify the perspective that most nearly corresponds to reality. This approach to ambiguity is essentially linear. Whatever mental abilities propel us on the most direct path from problem to resolution are viewed as adaptive. Although this direct path may vary from person to person, a global capacity to resolve problems, often measured in terms of speed, frequently serves as the operational definition of intelligence.[14]

What if categories such as "problem" and "resolution" are themselves assumptions that may or may not be useful? Rather than moving directly from problem to solution, a person in a mindful state remains open to several ways of viewing the situation. This flexibility allows us to draw on newly available information rather than to rely exclusively on preconstructed categories that tend to overdetermine our behavior. In other words, we have to maintain what some have called intelligent ignorance to make the best of any situation.

At this point, a skeptical reader may wonder whether, although we have demonstrated a mindful view of ambiguous two-dimensional figures, our actual environment is susceptible to such cartwheels. Consider a machine developed to spray crops. The manufacturer introduced the machine to farmers in Florida. Instead of helping to save the crops, the machine produced a substance that froze in the air and killed them. An entrepreneur viewed the same device from another perspective: he used it to make snow on northern ski slopes and earned a small fortune. A similar story involves the drug minoxidil, which was developed to lower blood pressure. Although it was effective for hypertension, minoxidil had a side effect: it stimulated hair growth. For a twenty-year-old woman, additional hair growth may be unwelcome, but for a balding man, renewed hair growth may be a blessing. From this perspective, hair growth was not a distressful side effect, but the principal element of the drug's success.

The discovery of new uses for these products did not begin with the problem of snowmaking or baldness. Rather, the discoveries occurred because the discoverers recognized that unsuccessful attempts to resolve problems could be seen from other perspectives. These mindful persons did not move in a linear way from problem to resolution; they moved from one perspective to another, from concern about side effects to a search for the promise of such effects. Had they rigidly continued to seek solutions for the original problems, they would have missed these alternative possibilities. As we will see in the next chapter on the illusion of right answers, side effects, or alternative solutions, would be considered wrong in a school setting.

Although flexible thinking is the essence of mindfulness, flexibility can also be considered a quality of intelligent thinking. We all have a repertoire of lower-level procedures and higher-level strategies that may be tried in novel settings. The larger our repertoire and the less we are attached to any specific procedure or strategy, the more flexible our thinking is likely to be. However, although our repertoire may grow, the individual strategies remain fixed. Our general capacity to sort through these various strategies and procedures and assess which can be applied most appropriately to a novel task is the process usually called intelligent thinking.[15]

In this view, intelligence consists of identifying the strategies and procedures that optimally reflect the context of any particular problem. Although this appears to be a more sophisticated view of intelligence, it is actually a return to the notion developed by Francis Galton and James Cattell, that intelligent thinking optimally corresponds to one's environment.

In contrast, when we are mindful, we are implicitly aware that in any particular situation there is no absolute optimum standard for action. *From a mindful perspective, one's response to a particular situation is not an attempt to make the best choice from among available options but to create options.* Rather than look for an external standard of optimum fit or the right answer, one discovers that, in the words of William James, "the standard perpetually grows up endogenously inside the web of experience."[16]

In ancient times the beautiful woman Mi Tzu-hsia was the favorite wife of the lord of Wei. Now, according to the law of Wei, anyone who rode in the king's carriage without permission could be punished by amputation of the foot. When Mi Tzu-hsia's mother fell ill, someone brought the news to her in the middle of the night. So she took the carriage and went out, and the king only praised her for it. "Such filial devotion!" he said. "For her mother's sake she risked the punishment of amputation!"

Another day she was dallying with the lord of Wei in the fruit garden. She took a peach, which she found so sweet that instead of finishing it she handed it to the lord to taste. "How she loves me," said the lord of Wei, "forgetting the pleasure of her own taste to share with me!"

But when Mi Tzu-hsia's beauty began to fade, the king's affection cooled. And when she offended the king, he prepared for her punishment, saying "Didn't she once take my carriage without permission? And didn't she once give me a peach that she had already chewed on?"

The King's Favorite
CHINESE FOLKTALE

Mi Tzu-hsia, like all of us, was dealing with an ever-shifting environment. She was so confident of the king's devotion that she did not protect herself against the possibility that circumstances could change. The lord of Wei, however, was bound by no such single perspective. While he clearly had the upper hand, perhaps an awareness of the possibility of shifting affections could have kept Mi Tzu-hsia in some control, more wary, more capable of ensuring her own survival.

7

The Illusion of Right Answers

There was once a poor man who had four sons, and when they were grown to manhood he said to them: "You will have to go out into the world, for I have nothing to give you. Be on your way, learn a trade, and see what you can make of yourselves." The four brothers took leave of their father and off they went, each in a different direction.

The eldest met a man who asked him where he was going. "I am going to learn a trade," he replied. "Come with me," said the man, "and learn to be a thief." "No," he said. "That does not pass as an honest trade nowadays. I'd only find myself dangling from the end of a rope." "Oh, you needn't worry," said the man. "I'll only teach you how to take things without ever being found out." That convinced him. He went with the man and became a skilled thief, so adroit that nothing he wanted was safe from him. The second brother met a man who also asked him what trade he had in mind. "I haven't decided yet," he replied. "Then come with me and learn to be a stargazer. There's no better trade, for nothing remains hidden from you." That appealed to him and he became so proficient a stargazer that when his apprenticeship was over, his master gave him a telescope, saying: "With this you will be able to see everything that happens on earth or in the heavens." A hunter took the third brother on as an apprentice and taught him all the tricks of the trade. As a farewell gift his master gave him a gun, saying: "It never misses. You will be sure to hit whatever you aim at." The youngest brother also met a tailor who offered to teach his trade. "Who wants to sit stooped over from morning to night, plying the needle and flatiron day in and day out?" said the boy. "You're only showing your ignorance," said the man. "With me you would learn tailoring of a different kind, which, in addition to being pleasant and dignified, may bring you great honor." That convinced him, so he went with the man and learned his craft from A to Z. As a farewell present, the man gave him a needle, saying: "With this you will be able to mend anything whatsoever, even if it's as soft as an egg or as hard as steel; two pieces will become as one, and no seam will be visible."

When the four years were over, the four brothers met at the crossroads, hugged and kissed each other, and went home eager for a chance to show their skills.

A few weeks later, the king's daughter was carried off by a dragon. The king worried day and night and made it known that the man who rescued his daughter and brought her back should have her for his wife. The brothers said to one another: "This is our chance."

The stargazer looked through his telescope and said, "I see her. She's sitting on a rock in the sea, far far away, and the dragon is right there guarding her." So he went to the king and asked for a ship for himself and his brothers, and they sailed across the sea until they came to the rock. There sat the king's daughter, and the dragon was lying asleep with his head in her lap. "I can't shoot," said the hunter, "for I'd kill the beautiful princess at the same time." "Then I'll see what I can do," said the thief. He crept up and stole her out from under the dragon, so deftly and quietly that the monster didn't notice a thing and went on snoring. Joyfully they ran back to the ship with her and headed for the open sea. But then the dragon woke up, found the king's daughter gone, and came flying through the air, fuming and snorting. He hovered over the ship and was just getting ready to swoop down, when the hunter took his gun and shot him straight through the heart. The dragon fell down dead, but his body was so big and heavy that it smashed the whole ship to pieces. Luckily, the brothers managed to grab hold of a few planks, which kept them and the princess afloat on the endless waters. They were in bad trouble, but without wasting a minute the tailor took his miraculous needle and sewed the planks together with a few big stitches. Then he sat down on his raft, collected the remaining parts of the ship and sewed them together so skillfully that they could all sail safely home.

When the king saw his daughter again, he was overjoyed and said to the four brothers: "One of you shall have her for his wife, but you will have to decide among yourselves which it is to be." At that a furious quarrel broke out, for each had his claim. The stargazer said:

"If I hadn't seen the king's daughter, all your skills would have been useless. Therefore she's mine." The thief said: "A lot of good your seeing her would have done if I hadn't stolen her out from under the dragon. Therefore she's mine." The hunter said: "The monster would have torn you all to pieces and the king's daughter with you, if my bullet hadn't killed it. Therefore she's mine." The tailor said: "If I hadn't repaired the ship with my needle, you'd all have drowned miserably. Therefore she's mine." The king replied: "You all have equal claims, but since you can't all marry my daughter, none of you shall have her, and instead I will reward you each with an equal part of a kingdom." That suited the brothers, who each settled down to enjoy the fortune he so rightly deserved.

> *The Four Artful Brothers*
> THE BROTHERS GRIMM
> (freely adapted)

The king wisely saw that each brother was right and wrong in his exclusive claim. Many of us, as students or teachers, are still in search of the one right answer. This belief in a single right answer rests on a view of intelligence that emphasizes outcomes and expert authority.

HOBBLED BY OUTCOMES

Intelligence is often seen as the capacity to achieve desirable outcomes. Arthur Jensen defends his concept of a general factor of intelligence by emphasizing its "practical validity for predicting the performance of individuals in school and college, in armed forces training programs, and in employment in business and industry."[1] Even Howard Gardner, proponent of a theory of multiple intelligences, describes intelligence as "an ability (or skill) to solve problems."[2] These and other theorists of intelligence presume that the goal of the educational process is to equip students to achieve specific, desirable outcomes.[3] An outcome's desirability, however, is dependent on context. An outcome that is good in one context may be most unwelcome in another.

The capacity to achieve an outcome is different from the ability to explore the world and understand experience. Trying to solve a math problem in a way dictated by the teacher is different from attempting to test one's own hypothesis. The teacher who tells students to solve a problem in a prescribed manner is limiting their ability to investigate their surroundings and to test novel ideas.

Much instruction tends to take a paint-by-number approach. Rather than allowing an individual to generate new hypotheses that may be mindfully tested in the individual's own experience, a teacher or expert often assumes that the objective is apparent and that only the means of achieving it remains obscure to the naive observer. Teaching from this perspective consists of presenting step-by-step methods of problem solving, making possible an essentially mindless type of success.

If we can shed this outcome orientation, we may discover that the freedom to define the process is more significant than achieving an outcome that has no inherent meaning or value outside that particular setting.

Even when intelligence theorists teach such global and frequently useful processes as inference making and hypothesis testing, they are still defining a valued outcome.[4] In this case the outcome is the acquisition of a particular set of skills. Such views can inhibit the capacity for exploring the skills best suited to an individual's goals.

This focus on skills is an attempt to mix traditional conceptions of intelligence as a general capacity with more skeptical views of intelligence as a product of socially acquired skills. Such a compromise is nonetheless outcome oriented. As Ann Brown and Joseph Campione have cogently argued, either one teaches specific skills—those valued in a particular context—or one teaches learning-to-learn skills."[5] These latter meta-abilities are defined by Brown and Campione as the student's speed in learning new tasks and ability to transfer this learning to other related tasks.

The definition of intelligence as learning-to-learn skills still is a traditional model: intelligence is the speed with which persons go from point A to point B. Intelligence testing, which focused first on such skills as bisecting lines or judging weights and later stressed problem solving, now emphasizes the *ability to acquire new skills*. In each case the objective—physical motion, problem resolution, or skill acquisition—is preselected by the intelligence expert.

When students are assessed in this way, they are not given an opportunity to choose their own objectives, nor are they allowed to explore processes that are outside the experts' repertoire of valued skills.

ACTOR/OBSERVER AND OTHER PERSPECTIVES

An expert's authority rests in large measure on an ability to predict events within an area of expertise more accurately than can a naive observer.[6] The ability to predict has been linked with perceptions of personal control.[7] It is possible to distinguish between two types of predictions. When experts make predictions, they generally rely on a collection of observations, sorted by categories that are believed to be stable over time. Yet all of us make predictions based on our own changing experience, not on observations of the behavior of others. The difference between a prediction generated from an actor's perspective (expert's prediction) and a prediction generated by an observer is crucial to understanding the distinction between the concepts of mindfulness and intelligence.[8]

An approach to problem solving based on traditional definitions of intelligence relies on the observer's capacity to use available data in constructing novel hypotheses that in turn reveal different perspectives on familiar questions. Those observers who have considerable familiarity with available data but have not yet become locked into a particular perspective are most likely to make conceptual contributions that advance our general understanding of an area of research.[9]

A mindful approach does not favor the observer's over the actor's perspective. We can test a hypothesis by applying it directly to our own behavior. As an informal example, an acquaintance had some plastic surgery on her face. Two days after the procedure she phoned the surgeon to say that the part of her earlobe that should be connected to her face was not. The surgeon, over the phone, said that was ridiculous; her husband, in her presence, agreed with the expert. Together they caused her to doubt her experience. However, she was stronger than many people in not denying her own reality. She returned to the doctor earlier than scheduled and insisted he look more closely at her ear. The event would have little meaning in this context, of course, if it had not turned out that she was right.

Consider now an example based on data. Much research in psychology has shown that people often ignore population-based information in favor of anecdotal, idiosyncratic information.[10] If, when car shopping, we are shown statistics underlining the high quality of a Volvo but we know someone who has had trouble with a Volvo, we are not likely to give much weight to the group-based information. Whether or not we accept given probabilities, we often don't think about who determined the base rate, that is, we don't consider what alternative probabilities could be if the issue were framed from other perspectives. This distinction can have far-reaching personal consequences. For example, a professor I know was being considered for tenure at a prestigious university. No one in her field had been tenured there for the past fifteen years, and no woman had ever been tenured there in that department. Friends and others outside the situation told her to look at the base rate, the probability of getting tenure in her department based on what had happened there in the past; their advice was to look for a position elsewhere. When she and I discussed her chances, I asked how many things she had attempted and successfully accomplished? That yielded a different probability for her potential success. We also looked up how many people tenured at the university had received their doctorates from the top school she had attended. That yielded yet another base rate. After trying these and other perspectives, she ended up following her instincts. As an aside, even if we believe there is only one base rate, which would make the probability here seem like zero, there is still a questionable assumption that the present is identical to the past; there is still the possibility of progress. Once again, everything is the same until it is not.

This professor received tenure, so this story had a happy ending, but it might not have. When our experience differs from that of the experts we can follow our own course or theirs and either one may yield a satisfying outcome or not. We cannot know in advance, or there would be no conflict to resolve. To my mind, there are advantages to following one's own perspective even when one loses. Mindful decision making, as opposed to decision making passively based on data assembled by outside observers, is a process of active self-definition.[11]

As we discussed in the context of ambiguous perceptual figures, our ability to view a situation from several perspectives may open a greater range of options. Shifting from ambiguous figures to the larger environment, we can see that the flexibility to change perspectives can open up options that would otherwise remain hidden. When we systematically attempt to narrow a choice, the perspective we most often neglect is our own experience.

Expert observers tend to focus on particular features of a situation that enable them to hold the variables constant. For example, a college admissions committee might admit to college those with the highest SAT scores and grade point averages (GPAs). Perceived stability is often in the experts' interest because their authority frequently rests on the stability of the categories they employ. If an admissions committee used a shifting variety of criteria for excellence, they might well lose their confidence in being able to distinguish the most desirable students. The individuals being rated, however, may be focusing on different, but significant criteria. For instance, consider a student whose grade improved from a C to an A or who achieved middling SAT scores despite having only recently learned English. When we rate our own behavior, it is often in our own interest to generate novel criteria. This capacity to find a means of shifting perspective can be a vital element of our ability to navigate new situations, just as the ability to maintain stable categories is often critical for the expert's authority.

Examples of the tendency of experts to use fixed categories when others might be more revealing can be found in many official educational assessments. Take the landmark *Equality of Educational Opportunity* report, which found that students' achievement was highly correlated with students' socioeconomic background but apparently uncorrelated with school quality.[12] This report has had an enormous impact on educational policy in the last twenty years. It led many educators to the disturbing conclusion that improving school quality would not increase students' level of achievement. Although this conclusion resulted in positive systemic changes, such as greater racial integration, it also created the unfortunate impression that educators who attempted to make changes in the schools apart from changing their socioeconomic makeup were misguided.

Later, research by Leigh Burstein and others revealed that factors that appeared to be unrelated on a national level were significantly correlated at an international level.[13] In this case, the shift in perspective was a change in what is called the unit of analysis. Unlike the earlier report, which focused only on differences among schools, Burstein's group focused on differences among school systems in several nations and found that educational decentralization, curricular differentiation, and selective tracking all increased the correlation between socioeconomic status and student achievement; tracking, as the name implies, kept the disadvantaged in place—they remained disadvantaged. More-centralized educational systems that offered a uniform curriculum without tracking reduced the effects of socioeconomic status on students' achievement.

Although social scientists recognize that applying statistical data derived from groups to individual cases is problematic, this recognition does not appear to restrict attempts to apply the perspectives developed through statistical methods to individuals.[14] An examination of the difference between focusing on group data and focusing on individual experience brings us back to the assumption that we questioned in Chapter 6, the belief that knowledge consists in knowing what's out there. Efforts to obtain quantified group data are constructed around the belief that these data most nearly *correspond* to reality and thus give individuals greater ability to predict future experience. From the observer's perspective, prediction, correspondence, and personal control are often viewed as synonymous.

From an actor's perspective, though, predictions based on an individual's experience may tend to become true for that individual. Such predictions may not correspond with reality as seen from an observer's perspective; nevertheless, they often prove valid for the actor.

This difference is illustrated in a study I undertook with colleagues several years ago.[15] We tested two distinct coping strategies designed to provide patients preparing to undergo major surgery with a greater experience of control as they entered the operating room. The first approach was based on the hypothesis that providing patients with information about pain and the recovery process based on statistical data would enhance their ability to predict what would happen to them and would enable them to experience greater personal control. Patients who were taught this coping strategy were provided with an objective account of preoperative procedures and with information, based on group data, about what they would most likely experience after the operation. Behind this hypothesis lies the assumption that information that most nearly corresponds to reality provides the greatest personal control.

In the second approach, patients were told that how they chose to view the surgical procedure was likely to determine how they would experience it. These patients were given ways in which to frame their experience. Being mindlessly sexist at the time, I first asked the male patients to imagine how they would respond to a minor cut in the context of playing football, and the female patients how they would respond while preparing to host a large dinner party. They were asked to contrast this imagined experience with that of receiving a minor cut while reading a boring newspaper. After considering how the context affected this imagined experience, patients were asked to think of instances when their perspective on an event had determined their experience of it. They were then asked to generate other perspectives for these same events. Finally, we worked with patients to construct a positive lens through which they could view their upcoming surgery.

We kept records of the percentage of patients who requested pain relievers and sedatives after their operations. Postoperative pain relievers were requested by a significantly smaller proportion of patients in the group that had been asked to view the surgery through a positive lens than in three other groups: (1) those given information based on group data, (2) those given both coping strategies, and (3) a no-treatment control group. Requests for postoperative sedatives followed the same pattern. These results indicate that although factual preparation and training in reframing both emphasize prediction as the key to an experience of personal control, the type of prediction offered by individual experience is distinct from the prediction offered by group data. Whereas prediction based on statistics assumes some correspondence with reality, prediction based on individual experience enables individuals to give meaning to their own future experience.

UNCERTAINTY AND CREATIVE THOUGHT

Although much of social science is an attempt to identify stable phenomena that can be generalized across time and to large groups, it is also interesting to examine the instability of experience as it differs from moment to moment and individual to individual.

Persons who dwell on this perceived instability are likely to experience greater uncertainty than those who dwell on fixed categories.[16] For some, such uncertainty represents an absence of personal control.[17] From a mindful perspective, however, uncertainty creates the freedom to discover meaning. If there are meaningful choices, there is uncertainty. If there is no choice, there is no uncertainty and no opportunity for control. The theory of mindfulness insists that uncertainty and the experience of personal control are inseparable.

Despite the tendency of uncertainty to enhance creative thinking, students are usually taught to view facts as immutable, unconditional truths. For instance, everyone knows that the sum of the angles of a triangle is 180 degrees. Students of geometry are not taught that this geometric theorem is derived from assumptions, assumptions that may be helpful in some contexts and less helpful in others, useful at some times and less useful at others. Imagine a child sitting on a carpeted floor as she measures the angles of a triangle with a protractor. The child painstakingly measures each angle and repeatedly finds that the sum of the angles equals 183 degrees. Her teacher, who knows better, is quick to remedy this problem. Because all intelligent and educated individuals have been taught that the sum of the angles must be 180 degrees, the teacher knows what to expect even before he measures the angles. Tolerant of the child's youthfulness and supportive of her budding empiricism, the teacher shows the child how to measure the angles correctly. True to the teacher's expectations, the measurements now come to exactly 180 degrees.

Having indulged the child's unformed intelligence, the teacher takes the opportunity to instruct the student on the facts of the matter. He informs the child that she need not measure the angles because geometers have proved that the sum of the angles must be 180 degrees. But the child, who is aware that her own angles were far more painstakingly measured than the teacher's, is not so easily beguiled.

She walks over to a globe and measures with her protractor the angle between the equator and the lines of longitude. They are all right angles, she says, 90 degrees. Then she traces a triangle with her finger: up from the equator to the North Pole and back down to the equator. Each of the lines of longitude forms a 90-degree angle with the equator, but they all meet at the North Pole. The child asks why there is a third angle at the North Pole when the two angles at the equator account for 180 degrees on their own.

We can anticipate the teacher's response: a triangle is a two-dimensional figure; it must be drawn on a flat surface; this triangle is on a curved surface and so is not really a triangle at all. But that is the point: the carpet on which the child measured the triangle earlier was also a curved surface. The perfectly flat surfaces of plane geometry are a mathematical abstraction, not an empirical reality. A small amount of variation in the surface of the carpet could easily account for the few additional degrees the child had carefully measured. It might also have provided a natural introduction to the geometry of curved surfaces, known as differential geometry. Yet the teacher was so constrained by his belief in truths independent of context that he failed to see this opportunity presented by a child measuring angles on a curved surface.

By mindfully considering data not as stable commodities but as sources of ambiguity, we become more observant. Consider the well-known sketch that may be viewed either as a vase or as two faces.[18] On first impression, an observer is likely to view the sketch as either one of these images but not as both. At this stage, most people are quite confident that the image is clear and even after lengthy inspection are not likely to see the other image. Only after being prompted to look at the sketch in another way does an observer see that what initially appeared as a vase appear as two faces.

The same drawing can be seen from a third perspective by turning it upside down. From this angle, the sketch might appear to be no more than a series of squiggles. Curiously, that is perhaps when we are looking most clearly. People usually depict figures more accurately when they copy forms from an inverted figure than when they copy directly.[19] It may be that by inverting the figure we free ourselves from preconceived categories and open ourselves to the available information—in this case, squiggles on a page.

When Right Becomes Wrong

Two quarreling men came to a judge. The first man told his story. The judge said, "That's right." His adversary, upset at the opinion, said, "You haven't heard my side of the story." He told his side and the judge said, "That's right." A third person said how can they both be right? The judge thought about it and said, "That's right."

One of the fears people may have of an educational system that creates a place for several perspectives is that nothing will remain stable, there will be nothing reliable on which they can lean for continuity. Yet we discover that by viewing the same information through several perspectives, we actually become more open to that information. The information may remain ambiguous, like the squiggles in our example, but we have a consistent foundation from which to work. Just as we might turn a figure upside down to copy it more accurately, we may view the same phenomenon from several perspectives to discover the information buried beneath our preconceived categories. If we fail to explore several perspectives, we risk confusing the stability of our own mindset with the stability of the phenomenon itself.

From time to time educators attempt to recognize the tremendous fluidity of knowledge by providing students with a list of the pros and cons of a particular idea or theory. Much as a physician might list the potential negative side effects along with the expected benefits of a treatment, critical thinking is sometimes taught in schools by having students list the advantages and disadvantages of a controversial idea. Such an exercise almost invariably falls short of the recognition that each potential benefit may also be a liability and that a disadvantage may become an advantage.

Galileo embodied this ambiguity in human accomplishments. Galileo relied on direct observation to transform the nature of truth in Western culture. Empiricism is commonplace today, but for Galileo's contemporaries it was a novelty. The vast majority of Galileo's contemporaries, following Aristotle, believed that a heavier object would fall more quickly than a lighter object. Galileo demonstrated that, if one could account for differences in air resistance, objects of unequal weight would fall at the same rate. He overturned the worldview that dominated his age merely by testing it empirically.

Yet we may also see Galileo as a person trapped by his own ideas. Insisting that only what could be seen was believable, Galileo dismissed the work of his contemporary Johannes Kepler. From Galileo's perspective Kepler relied on a mysterious, unseen and therefore unbelievable force. Today this force is called gravity. By discounting Kepler's assertion that the moon caused the tides, Galileo failed to recognize a force that today is considered self-evident. Galileo's strength, his reliance on direct observation, also proved to have limitations.

Those of us who teach are often tolerant of students' mistakes—especially when we believe that the students are of limited intelligence—but it does not occur to us to view their answers not as mistakes, but as responses to a different context.

To view an answer as right or wrong, we must freeze the context in which the answer is being evaluated. Take, for example, "The shortest distance between two points is a straight path." This statement might be right in the context of plane geometry, but try to get to the bank from your home and note the quickest way. As another example, try fitting the equation 2 + 2 = 4 with "The whole is greater than the sum of its parts."

When we are mindful, we recognize that every inadequate answer is adequate in another context. In the perspective of every person lies a lens through which we may better understand ourselves. If we respect students' abilities to define their own experiences, to generate their own hypotheses, and to discover new ways of categorizing the world, we might not be so quick to evaluate the adequacy of their answers. We might, instead, begin listening to their questions. Out of the questions of students come some of the most creative ideas and discoveries.

MINDFULNESS AND SELF-DEFINITION

Perhaps it was because of a desire to provide at least one dimension on which each person could compare favorably that

J. P. Guilford developed a model of intelligence having 150 distinct dimensions. He hoped that this model would be useful "in guiding students into courses and majors" and "pointing to undemonstrated abilities."[20]

Although the proliferation of dimensions of intelligence may help prop up students' sense of self-worth, in the process of identifying strengths we may be unintentionally undermining students' development. Not only do the students who are helped lose the potential benefit of generating a view of their own abilities, but the recipients of most remedial efforts usually accept a devaluation of self.[21] Such devaluation sometimes causes people to compensate by devaluing others. In other words, people accept the ways others have been shown to be better than they by identifying ways in which they are better than others.[22] Adding dimensions of intelligence encourages such labeling and competition.

Such comparisons may also lead to devaluing certain aspects of experience in order to draw comparisons that are personally favorable. People tend to value activities that they do well and to devalue activities at which they are not successful.

From their inception intelligence tests have encouraged this negative labeling. They have been used to identify students who would benefit from programs other than the normal school curriculum. The first intelligence test was developed to assist the French Ministry of Education in identifying students who needed to be placed in remedial schools. We continue to view testing of intelligence as a means of sorting students into groups of one kind or another: college bound, vocational, gifted, and so on. Too often, rather than encouraging students to discover the usefulness of their failures or to identify the abilities embedded in their disabilities, our educational system seeks to help students by steering them in directions that avoid such challenges.

By valuing some activities—subjects, sports, courses—and devaluing others, we ignore the many perspectives from which any activity may be viewed. At every moment in a mindful state, we are learning something, we are changing in some way, we are interacting with the environment so that both we and the environment are changed. From this perspective, a moment spent on one activity as opposed to another is not consequential. Once we realize that whenever we tackle any particular task we are learning and growing, we do not measure ourselves by the type or program or course we are in. By the same token, once we realize that the reason we did not accomplish one task was because another task *was* accomplished, we no longer need to evaluate ourselves negatively for not accomplishing the first task.[23]

LEARNING AS RE-IMAGINING THE WORLD

As we saw earlier, at the heart of many theories of intelligence is a belief that it is possible to identify an optimum fit between individual and environment. However, we can see that how we interact with our environment is not a matter of fitting ourselves to an external norm; rather, it is a process by which we give form, meaning, and value to our world. If there is no best fit, then an ability to identify an optimum fit may not be a useful concept.

137

I do not mean to suggest that intelligence tests do not measure something, but the dimension these tests measure may be a neutral trait. The abilities measured by intelligence tests may be useful in certain situations, much as it is sometimes useful to be tall. Yet being small, although burdensome in an environment constructed for taller people, could be an advantage for working in certain conditions, and it is not difficult to imagine a world in which tallness would be a disadvantage. If the world had been designed by small people, imagine how uncomfortable others would be. It is more difficult to imagine an environment in which low intelligence would be advantageous. Nonetheless, mindfulness theory asks us to imagine it. The degree to which we are unable to do so is an an indication of how comprehensively our world has been organized around the category of intelligence.

When shown a sentence with a word repeated in it, people almost always miss the extra word. For instance, try out the last sentence of the preceding paragraph on your friends or colleagues. When a small group of people with head injuries was shown such a sentence, all of them caught the double word, *an* in the example. Why is this so? We can only hypothesize that those who have lost some of their familiar abilities are no longer able to take the world for granted. (Experienced meditators also found the double word with no problem.)

Any disability may function as an ability if we are able to view it from a new perspective.[24] When we are mindful, we recognize that the way in which we tend to construct our world is only one construction among many. We might consider reconstructing this world for ourselves whenever it does not fit our abilities or perceived lack of abilities, whenever we feel stunted or less than fully effective. From a mindful perspective, when we are not feeling smart we are not being stupid; rather, we are being sensible from some other perspective. Even when we are feeling brilliant, we still have a lot to learn from those of so-called low intelligence about alternative ways of constructing our world.

The widespread failure to recognize the insights that can be found in all different perspectives may itself constitute a disability. Indeed, those of us who are intelligent enough to be writing or reading about such an abstract concept as intelligence may suffer severely from this disability. Should we continue to teach this disability to our children?

One day Soshi was walking on the bank of a river with a friend. "How delightfully the fishes are enjoying themselves in the water," exclaimed Soshi. His friend spoke to him thus, "You are not a fish, how do you know that the fishes are enjoying themselves?" "You are not myself," returned Soshi, "how do you know that I do not know that the fishes are enjoying themselves?"

KAKUZO OKAKURA
Japanese Philosopher

How can we know if we do not ask? Why should we ask if we are certain we know? All answers come out of the question. If we pay attention to our questions, we increase the power of mindful learning.

Notes

INTRODUCTION

1. *New York Times Magazine,* August 11, 1996.

2. Langer, E. *Mindfulness.* Reading, MA: Addison-Wesley, 1989.

1 WHEN PRACTICE MAKES IMPERFECT

1. Saint-Exupéry, A. de. *The Little Prince,* trans. Katherine Woods (New York: Harcourt Brace, 1943, 1971).

2. Langer, E., and Imber, L. "When Practice Makes Imperfect: The Debilitating Effects of Overlearning, *Journal of Personality and Social Psychology* 37 (1979): 2014–25.

3. Dudkin, D., Brandt, D., Bodner, T., and Langer, E., unpublished data, Harvard University.

4. Langer, E., *Mindfulness* (Reading, MA: Addison-Wesley, 1989).

5. Milgram, S., *Obedience to Authority* (New York: Harper and Row, 1974).

6. Pietrasz, L. and Langer, E., unpublished manuscript (Harvard University).

7. Langer, E., *Mindfulness* (Reading, MA: Addison-Wesley, 1989).

8. Pierce, A., and Pierce, R., *Expressive Movement: Posture and Action in Daily Life, Sports and the Performing Arts* (New York: Plenum Press, 1989).

9. Feldman, D., *Nature's Gambit: Child Prodigies and the Development of Human Potential* (New York: Basic Books, 1986).

10. Anderson J. R., *Cognitive Science and It's Implications* (San Francisco: W. H. Freeman, 1980).

11. Payzant, G. *Glenn Gould, Music and Mind* (Toronto: Key Porter Books, 1984).

12. Bodner, T., Waterfield, R., and Langer, E., "Mindfulness in Finance" (manuscript in preparation, Harvard University).

2 CREATIVE DISTRACTION

1. Langer, E., Janis, I., and Wolfer, J., "Reduction of Psychological Stress in Surgical Patients," *Journal of Experimental Psychology* 11 (1975): 155–65.

2. Yarbus, A. L. *Role of Eye Movements in the Visual Process* (Nauka: Moscow, 1965).

3. Langer, E., and Bodner, T., "Mindfulness and Attention" (manuscript, Harvard University, 1995).

4. Langer, E., and Bayliss, M., "Mindfulness, Attention, and Memory" (manuscript, Harvard University, 1994).

5. American Psychiatric Association, DSM IV Washington, DC, 1994 (also APA WWW page on Childhood Disorders); "Attention Deficit Hyperactivity Disorder" (Rockville, MD: National Institute of Mental Health, 1994).

6. Batshaw, M. L., and Perret, Y. M., *Children with Disabilities: A Medical Primer* (Baltimore: P. H. Brooks, 1992).

7. Levy, B., "The Dopamine Theory of Attention Deficit Hyperactivity Disorder (ADHD)," *Australian and New Zealand Journal of Psychiatry* 25(2), (1991), 277–83; Lou, H. C., Henriksen, L., and Bruhn, P., "Focal Cerebral Dysfunction in Developmental Learning Disabilities," *The Lancet* 335, no. 8680 (Jan. 1990): 8; Zametkin, A. J., Nordahl, T. E., Gross, M., King, C. A., et al. "Cerebral Glucose Metabolism in Adults with Hyperactivity of Childhood Onset," *New England Journal of Medicine* 323, no. 20 (Nov. 1990): 1361–66.

8. Vyse, S. A., and Rapport, M. D. "The Effects of Methylphenidate on Learning in Children with ADHD: The Stimulus Equivalence Paradigm," *Journal of Consultation and Clinical Psychology* 57, no. 3 (June 1989): 425–35.

9. Landau, S., Lorch, E. P., and Milich, R., "Visual Attention to and Comprehension of Television in Attention-Deficit Hyperactivity Disordered and Normal Boys," *Child Development* 63 no. 4 (Aug. 1992): 928–37.

10. Ford, M., Poe, V., and Cox, J. "Attending Behaviors of ADHD Children in Math and Reading Using Various Types

of Software," *Journal of Computing in Childhood Education 4,* no. 2 (1993): 183–96.

11. Cripe, F. F., "Rock Music as Therapy for Children with Attention Deficit Disorder: An Exploratory Study," *Journal of Music Therapy* 23, no. 1 (Spring 1986): 30–37.

12. Zentall, S. S., "The Attraction of Color for Active Attention-Problem Children." *Exceptional Children* 54, no. 4 (Jan. 1988): 357–62.

13. Carson, S., Shih, M., and Langer, E. "Sit Still and Pay Attention?" (manuscript, Harvard University, 1996).

3 THE MYTH OF DELAYED GRATIFICATION

1. Lerner, M., Miller, D., and Holmes, J. "Deserving versus Justice: A Contemporary Dilemma," in *Advances in Experimental Social Psychology*, ed. L. Berkowitz, vol. 9 (New York: Academic Press, 1976).

2. Deci, E., "Effects of Externally Mediated Rewards on Intrinsic Motivation," *Journal of Personality and Social Psychology* 18 (1971): 105–15; Kruglanski, A., Freedman, I., and Zeevi, G., "The Effect of Extrinsic Incentive on Some Qualitative Aspects of Task Performance," *Journal of Personality* 39 (1971): 606–17; Lepper, M., Greene, D., and Nisbett, R., "Undermining Children's Intrinsic Interest with Extrinsic Reward: A Test of the Overjustification Hypothesis," *Journal of Personality and Social Psychology* 28 (1973): 129–38; Pittman, T., and Heller, J., "Social Motivation," *Annual Review of Psychology* 38 (1987): 461–89.

3. Steele, C. M., and Aronson, J. "Stereotype Threat and the Intellectual Test Performance of African Americans," *Journal*

of Personality and Social Psychology 69, no. 5 (Nov. 1995): 797–811.

4. Snow, S., and Langer, E., unpublished data. Harvard University.

5. LeVine, R. Personal communication.

6. Langer, E., and Pietrasz, L., "From Reference to Preference" (manuscript, Harvard University, 1995).

7. Marcus, A., and Langer, E., "Mindfulness as a Means of Reducing Conformity" (manuscript, Harvard University, 1990).

8. Zajonc, R., "Attributional Effects of Mere Exposure," *Journal of Personality and Social Psychology* 9, suppl. no. 2, part 2 (1968).

9. Bornstein, R. F., "Exposure and Affect: An Overview and Meta-Analysis of Research, 1968–1987," *Psychological Bulletin* 106, no. 2 (1989): 265–89.

10. Saegart, S. C., and Jellison, J. M., "Effects of Initial Level of Response Competition and Frequency of Exposure on Liking and Exploratory Behavior," *Journal of Personality and Social Psychology* 16 (1970): 553–58.

11. Langer, E., Bashner, R., and Chanowitz, B., "Decreasing Prejudice by Increasing Discrimination," *Journal of Personality and Social Psychology* 49 (1985): 113–20.

4   1066 WHAT? OR THE HAZARDS
OF ROTE MEMORY

1. Noice, H., "The Role of Explanations and Plan Recognition in the Learning of Theatrical Scripts," *Cognitive Science* 15 (1991): 425–60; Anderson, J., and Reder, L., "An Elaborate Pro-

cessing of Depth of Processing," in *Levels of Processing in Human Memory*, ed. L. Cerrick and F. Craik (Hillsdale, NJ: Erlbaum, 1979), 385–403; Hilgard, E., and Marquis, D. G., *Conditioning and Learning* (New York: Appleton-Century-Crofts, 1961).

2. MacIver, D. J., and Epstein, J. L., "Impact of Algebra-Focused Course Content and Active Learning/Teaching for Understanding Instructional Approaches on Eighth-Graders' Achievement" (Baltimore, MD: Johns Hopkins University Center for Social Organization of Schools. Disadv. Stud., 1994).

3. Becker, H. J., "Mathematics With Meaning" (Baltimore, MD: Johns Hopkins University Center for Social Organization of Schools. 1993).

4. Rutherford, F. J., and Ahlgren, A., *Science for All Americans* (New York: Oxford University Press, 1990).

5. Bereiter C., and Scardamalia, M. (1987), "An Attainable Version of High Literacy: Approaches to Teaching Higher-Order Thinking Skills in Reading and Writing," *Curriculum Inquirer* 17(1987): 9–30.

6. Epstein, J. L., and Salinas, K. C., *Promising Programs in the Middle Grades* (Reston, VA: National Association of Secondary School Principals, 1992).

7. Raudenbush, S. W., Rowan, B., and Cheong, Y. F., "Higher Order Instructional Goals in Secondary Schools: Class, Teacher, and School Influences," *American Educational Research Journal* 20, no. 3 (1993): 523–53.

8. Markus, H., "Self-Schemata and Processing Information about the Self," *Journal of Personality and Social Psychology* 35 (1977): 63–78; Rogers, T., Kuiper, N., and Kirker, W., "Self-

Reference and the Encoding of Personal Information," *Journal of Personality and Social Psychology* 35 (1977): 677–88.

9. Markus, H., Crane, M., Bernstein, S., and Siladi, N., "Self-Schemas and Gender," *Journal of Personality and Social Psychology* 42 (1982): 38–50.

10. Bellezza, F. S., "The Self as a Mnemonic Device: The Role of Internal Cues." *Journal of Personality and Social Psychology* 3 (1984): 47.

11. Noice, H., "The Role of Explanation and Plan Recognition in the Learning of Theatrical Scripts," *Cognitive Science* 15 (1991): 425–460.

12. Lieberman, M., and Langer, E. 1995 "Mindfulness and the Process of Learning," in *Learning and Context*, ed. P. Antonacci (Cresskill, NJ: Hampton Press, 1995).

13. Ibid.

14. Mueller, C., and Langer, E., "Encoding Variability and Mindfulness" (manuscript, Harvard University, 1995).

15. Eck, J., "Medical Misdiagnosis with the Elderly" (ALM thesis, Harvard University Extension School, 1994).

5 A New Look at Forgetting

1. Dror, I, and Langer, E. "The Danger of Knowing Too Much: Cognitive Plasticity and Knowledge," in *Creativity and Cognition* (in preparation).

2. Maier, N. R. F., "Reasoning in Humans II: The Solution of a Problem and its Appearance in Consciousness," *Journal of*

Comparative Psychology 12 (1931): 181–194; Duncker, K., "Part Three: Fixedness of Thought Material," *Psychological Monographs* 58 (1945): 85–111; Langer, E., and Weinman, C. "When Thinking Disrupts Intellectual Performance: Mindlessness on an Overlearned Task," *Personality and Social Psychology Bulletin* 7 (1981): 240–43 (1981); Condoor, S. S., Brock, H. R., and Burger, C. D., "Innovation Through Early Recognition of Critical Design Parameters," Paper presented at the meeting of the ASEE, Urbana, Illinois, June 1993; Hecht, H., and Profitt, D. R., "The Price of Expertise: Effects of Experience on the Water-Level Task," *Journal of Psychological Science* 6 (2) (1995): 90–95.

3. Moore, B., Sherrod, D., Liu, T., Underwood, B., "The Dispositional Shift in Attribution over Time," *Journal of Experimental Social Psychology* 15 no. 6 (1979): 553–69.

4. Estes, W. K. "Is Human Memory Obsolete?" *American Scientist* 68 (1980): 62–69.

Pratkanis, A. R., Greenwald, A. G., Leippe, M. R., and Baumgardner, M. H. "In Search of Reliable Persuasion Effects: III. The Sleeper Effect Is Dead: Long Live the Sleeper Effect." *Journal of Personality and Social Psychology* 54 (1988): 203–18.

Schacter, D. L., Harbluk, J. L., and McLachlan, D. R. "Retrieved Without Recollection: An Experimental Analysis of Source Amnesia," *Journal of Verbal Learning and Verbal Behavior* 23 (1984): 593–611.

5. Cutler, S., and Grams, A., "Correlates of Self-Reported Everyday Memory Problems," *Journal of Gerontology: Social Sciences* 43 (1988): 582–90; Palmore, E., *Facts on Aging Quiz: A Handbook of Uses and Results* (New York: Springer, 1988);

Ryan, E., "Beliefs about Memory across the Life Span," *Journal of Gerontology: Psychological Sciences* 47 (1992): 41–47.

6. Baddeley, A. *Working Memory* (Oxford, England: Clarendon, 1986); Johansson, B., Zarit, S., and Berg, S., "Changes in Cognitive Functioning of the Oldest Old," *Journal of Gerontology: Psychological Sciences* 47 (1992): 75–80; Light, L., and Burke, D., "Patterns of Language and Memory in Old Age," in *Language, Memory and Aging*, ed. L. Light and D. Burke (New York: Cambridge University Press, 1988), 244–71.

7. Holland, C., and Rabbit, P., "Effects of Age-Related Reductions in Processing Resources on Text Recall," *Journal of Gerontology: Psychological Sciences* 47 (1992): 129–37; Langer, E., Rodin, J., Beck, P., Weinman, C., and Spitzer, L., "Environmental Determinants of Memory Improvement in Late Adulthood," *Journal of Personality and Social Psychology* 37 (1979): 2003–13; Rissenberg, M., and Glanzer, M., "Picture Superiority in Free Recall: The Effects of Normal Aging and Primary Degenerative Dementia," *Journal of Gerontology: Psychological Sciences* 41 (1986): 64–71.

8. Kite, M., and Johnson, B., "Attitudes toward Older and Younger Adults: A Meta-analysis," *Psychology and Aging* 3 (1988): 233–44.

9. Perdue, C., and Gurtman, M., "Evidence for the Automaticity of Ageism," *Journal of Experimental Social Psychology* 26 (1990): 199–216.

10. Langer, E., *Mindfulness* (Reading, MA: Addison-Wesley, 1989).

11. Ibid.

12. Levy, B., and Langer, E., "Memory Advantage for Deaf and Chinese Elders: Aging Free from Negative Premature Cognitive Commitments," *Journal of Personality and Social Psychology* 66, no. 6 (Jan. 1994): 989–97.

13. Becker, H. J., *Growing Old in Silence* (Berkeley: University of California Press, 1980); Davis, D. *Long Lives: Chinese Elderly and the Communist Revolution* (Cambridge: Harvard University Press, 1983); Ikels, C., "Aging and Disability in China: Cultural Issues in Measurement and Interpretation," *Social Science and Medicine* 32 (1991): 649–65; Padden, C., and Humphries, T., *Deaf in America: Voices from a Culture* (Cambridge: Harvard University Press, 1988).

14. Higgins, P., *Outsiders in a Hearing World: A Sociology of Deafness* (Beverly Hills, CA: Sage, 1980); Padden and Humphries, *Deaf in America*.

15. Becker, H. J., *Growing Old in Silence*.

16. Hall, S., "Train-Gone-Sorry: The Etiquette of Social Conversations in American Sign Language," in *American Deaf Culture: An Anthology*, ed. S. Wilcox (Silver Spring, MD: Linstok, 1989), 89–102.

17. Becker, H. J., *Growing Old in Silence*; Padden and Humphries, *Deaf in America*.

18. Davis, *Long Lives*; Sher, A., *Aging in Post-Mao China: The Politics of Veneration* (Boulder, CO: Westview Press, 1984).

19. Davis, *Long Lives*.

20. Ikels, C., "New Options for the Urban Elderly," in *Chinese Society on the Eve of Tiananmen: The Impact of Reform*, ed.

D. Davis and E. Vogel (Cambridge: The Harvard University Council of East Asian Studies, 1990), 214–42; Sher, *Aging*.

21. Davis, *Long Lives*; Ikels, "Aging and Disability."

22. Furth, H., *Thinking without Language: Psychological Implications of Deafness* (New York: Free Press, 1966); Jacobs, L., *A Deaf Adult Speaks Out* (Washington, DC: Gallaudet University Press, 1969); Padden and Humphries, *Deaf in America*.

23. Ikels, C, "New Options."

24. Becker, *Growing Old in Silence*.

25. Rosenthal, R., and Jacobson, L., *Pygmalion in the Classroom* (New York: Holt, Rinehart, and Winston, 1968).

6 MINDFULNESS AND INTELLIGENCE

1. Spearman, C., *The Abilities of Man* (New York: Macmillan, 1997).

2. Gardner, H., *Frames of Mind: The Theory of Multiple Intelligences* (New York: Basic Books, 1983), 2, 7.

3. Goleman, D., *Emotional Intelligence* (New York: Bantam Books, 1995).

4. Helmholtz, H. L., *Handbuch der physiologischen Optik* (Helmholtz's treatise on physiological optics), trans. J. P. C. Southall (Rochester, NY: The Optical Society of America, 1924), 3.

5. Boring, E. G., *A History of Experimental Psychology* (Englewood Cliffs, NJ: Prentice-Hall, 1950).

6. Darwin, C., *Expressions of the Emotions in Man and Animals* (New York: Appleton-Century-Crofts, 1873).

7. Spencer, H., *Principles of Psychology* (New York: Appleton, 1883).

8. Thorndike, E. L., *Selected Writings from a Connectionalist's Psychology* (New York: Appleton-Century-Crofts,1949).

9. Ibid.

10. Cattell, R. B., *Intelligence: Its Structure, Growth and Action* (Amsterdam: Elsevier, 1987); Gardner, H., *Frames of Mind*; Horn, J., "Intellectual Ability Concepts," *Advances in the Psychology of Human Intelligence* 3 (1986): 35–77; Sternberg, R. J., *Beyond IQ: A Triarchic Theory of Human Intelligence* (Cambridge: Cambridge University Press, 1985); Sternberg, R. J., "Domain-Generality versus Domain-Specificity: The Life of Impending Death of a False Dichotomy," *Merrill–Palmer Quarterly* 35, no. 1 (1989): 115–30.

11. Sternberg, *Beyond IQ*.

12. James, W., *The Meaning of Truth* (Cambridge: Harvard University Press, 1878).

13. Dixon, R. A., Kramer, D. A., and Baltes, P. B., "Intelligence: A Life-Span Developmental Perspective," in *Handbook of Intelligence: Theories, Measurements and Applications*, ed. B. B. Wolman (New York: John Wiley and Sons, 1985), 301–50.

14. Eysenck, H. J., "A General Systems Approach to the Measurement of Intelligence and Personality," in *Intelligence and Cognition: Contemporary Frames of Reference*, ed. S. H. Irvine and S. E. Newstead (Dordrecht, Netherlands: Marti-

nus Nijhoff, 1987), 349–75; Jensen, A. R., "Reaction Time and Psychometric g," in *A Model for Intelligence*, ed. H. J. Eysenck (New York: Springer, 1982), 93–132; Sternberg, R. J., "Representation and Process in Linear Syllogistic Reasoning," *Journal of Experimental Psychology: General* 109 (1980): 119–59.

15. Frensch, P. A., and Sternberg, R. J., "Expertise and Intelligent Thinking: When Is It Worse to Know Better?" *Advances in the Psychology of Human Intelligence* 3 (1989): 157–88.

16. James, *The Meaning of Truth.*

7 THE ILLUSION OF RIGHT ANSWERS

1. Jensen, A. R. "Intelligence: Definition, Measurement, and Future Research," in *What Is Intelligence?: Contemporary Viewpoints on Its Nature and Definition*, ed. R. J. Sternberg and D. K. Detterman (Norwood, NJ: Ablex Publishing, 1986), 109–12.

2. Gardner, H., "The Waning of Intelligence Tests," in *What Is Intelligence?: Contemporary Viewpoints on Its Nature and Definition*, ed. R. J. Sternberg and D. K. Detterman (Norwood, NJ: Ablex Publishing, 1986), 73–76.

3. Brown, A. L., and Campione, J. C., "Modifying Intelligence or Modifying Skills: More Than a Semantic Quibble?" in *How and How Much Can Intelligence Be Increased*, ed. D. K. Detterman and R. J. Sternberg (Norwood, NJ: Ablex Publishing, 1982), 215–30.

4. Collins, A., and Smith, E. E., "Teaching the Process of Reading Comprehension," in *How and How Much Can Intelli-*

gence Be Increased, ed. D. K. Detterman and R. J. Sternberg (Norwood, NJ: Ablex Publishing, 1982), 173–85.

5. Brown, and Campione, "Modifying Intelligence."

6. Lichenstein, S., Fischhoff, B., and Phillips, L. D., "Calibration of Probabilities: The State of the Art to 1980," in *Judgment Under Uncertainty: Heuristics and Biases*, ed. D. Kahneman, P. Slovic, and A. Tversky (Cambridge: Cambridge University Press, 1982), 306–34.

7. Langer, E., "The Illusion of Control," *Journal of Personality and Social Psychology* 32, no. 2 (1975): 311–28.

8. Jones, E., and Nisbett, R., "The Actor and the Observer: Divergent Perceptions of the Causes of Behavior," in *Attribution: Perceiving the Causes of Behavior*, ed. E. Jones (Morristown, NJ: General Learning Press, 1972), 74–94.

9. Frensch, P. A., and Sternberg, R. J., "Expertise and Intelligent Thinking: When Is It Worse to Know Better?" *Advances in the Psychology of Human Intelligence* 3 (1989): 157–88.

10. Kahneman, D., and Tversky, A., "A Heuristic for Judging Frequency and Probability," *Cognitive Psychology* 5, no. 2 (Sept. 1973): 207–32; Kahneman, D., and Tversky, A., "On the Psychology of Prediction," *Psychological Review* 80, no. 4 (July 1973): 237–51.

11. Langer, E., "The Illusion of Calculated Decisions," in *Beliefs, Reasoning and Decision Making*, ed. R. Schank and E. Langer (Hillsdale, NJ: Erlbaum, 1994).

12. Coleman, J. S., Campbell, E. Q., Holson, C. J., McPartland, J., Mood, A., Weinfeld, E. D., and York, R. L., *Equality of Educational Opportunity* (Washington, DC: U.S.P.O., 1966).

13. Burstein, L., Fisher, K. B., and Miller, M. D., "The Multi-level Effects of Background in Science Achievement: A Cross-national Comparison," *Sociology of Education* 53 (1980): 215–25.

14. De Rivera, J., *Field Theory as Human Science: Contributions of Lewin's Berlin Group* (New York: Gardner Press, 1976).

15. Langer, E., Janis, I. L., and Wolfer, J. A., "Reduction of Psychological Stress in Surgical Patients," *Journal of Experimental Social Psychology* 11 (1975): 155–65.

16. Langer, E., *Mindfulness* (Reading, MA: Addison-Wesley, 1989), 2, 8; Cantor, N., and Kihlstrom, J. F., *Personality and Social Intelligence* (Englewood Cliffs, NJ: Prentice-Hall, 1987).

17. Staub, E., Tursky, B., and Schwartz, G. E., "Self-Control and Predictability: The Effects of Reactions to Aversive Stimulation," *Journal of Personality and Social Psychology* 18, no. 2 (1971): 157–62.

18. Edwards, B., *Drawing on the Right Side of the Brain* (Los Angeles: J. P. Tarcher, 1979), 12, 13.

19. Ibid.

20. Guilford, J. P., "The Structure-of-Intellect Model," in *Handbook of Intelligence: Theories, Measurements and Applications*, ed. B. B. Wolman (New York: John Wiley & Sons, 1985), 225–66.

21. Langer, E., and Benevento, A., "Self-Induced Dependence," *Journal of Personality and Social Psychology* 36, no. 8 (Aug. 1978): 886–93; Langer, E., and Avorn, J., "Induced Disability in Nursing Home Patients: A Controlled Trial," *Journal of the American Geriatric Society* 30, no. 6 (1981): 397–400;

Steele, C. M., and Aronson, J., "Stereotype Threat and the Intellectual Test Performance of African Americans," *Journal of Personality and Social Psychology* 69, no. 5 (1995): 797–811.

22. Taylor, S. E. Wood, J., and Lichtman, R., "It Could Be Worse: Selective Evaluation as a Response to Victimization," *Journal of Social Issues* 39 no. 2 (1984): 19–40; Wills, T. A., "Social Comparison in Coping and Help-Seeking," in *New Directions in Helping*, ed. B. M. DePaulo, A. Nadler, and J. D. Fisher, vol. 2, *Help-Seeking* (New York: Academic Press, 1983), 109–141.

23. Langer, E., "The Illusion of Incompetence," in *Choice and Perceived Control*, ed. L. C. Perlmuter and R. A. Monty (Hillsdale, NJ: Erlbaum, 1979), 301–13; Langer, E., and Park, K., "Incompetence: A Conceptual Reconsideration," in *Competence Considered*, ed. R. J. Sternberg and J. Kolligian (New Haven, CT: Yale University Press, 1990), 149–66.

24. Langer, E., and Chanowitz, B., "A New Perspective for the Study of Disability," in *Attitudes Towards Persons with Disabilities*, ed. H. E. Yuker (New York: Springer, 1987), 68–81; Langer, and Park, "Incompetence," in *Competence Considered*, ed. R. J. Sternberg and J. Kolligian (New Haven, CT: Yale University Press, 1990), 149–66.

Index

A

Absolute, versus conditional learning, 79–81
Activities/tasks
  making distinctions, 59–60
  perspectives, mindful learning and, 136–37
Actor/observer and other perspectives, right answers and, 123–30
Age, aging
  attitudes/stereotypes towards, 91–92, 93, 95
  memory, alternative views of, 93–98
  memory decline in, 90–93
  mindfulness, life expectancy and, 4
Ahlgren, A., 146
Alexander, Charles, 157
Ambiguity
  right answers and, 133–35
  tolerance for, 63–64
American Psychiatric Association, 143

Anderson, J., 142, 145
Anderson, Norman, 26
Anticipation, delayed gratification and, 54–55
Aristotle, 134
Aronson, J., 144, 155
Associative stage, in learning a new skill, 26
Assumptions
  about "facts," 19–20, 71
  about intelligence, 127
  about work and play, 52–56
  context, uncertainty and, 130–31
Attention/attentiveness
  difficulties with, 37–40
  distraction and, 35–37
  learning myth about, 2, 33–35
  meanings attached to, 38
  novelty and, 40–43
  soft vigilance and, 43–44
Attention deficit hyperactivity disorder (ADHD), 6–7, 37, 44–49
Authority, obedience to, experiment in, 20–21

Autonomous stage, learning a new
   skill, 26
Avorn, J., 19, 155

B

Baddeley, A., 149
Baltes, P.B., 152
Bashner, R., 64, 145
Basic skills, practice of
   context, uncertainty, doubt and,
      15–22
   learning myth about, 2, 10
   memorization and, 73
   mindful learning and, 22–28
   overlearned, 11–14, 17
   sideways learning, 22–28
Batshaw, M.L., 143
Baumgardner, M.H., 148
Bayliss, M., 41, 143
Beck, P., 149
Becker, H.J., 146, 150–51
Beethoven, Ludwig van, 27
Bellezza, F.S., 147
Benevento, A., 155
Bereiter, C., 146
Berg, S., 148
Bernstein, S., 147
Binet, Alfred, 104
Binet-Simon Intelligence Test,
   104
Bishop, Elizabeth, *The Collected
   Prose*, 51
Bodner, T., 18, 28, 40, 141, 142
Boredom
   mere exposure effect and, 64
   rote memorization and, 71
Boring, E.G., 151
Bornstein, R.F., 145

Bottom-up teaching method, 22
Brandt, D., 18, 141
Breathing, attentiveness and, 39
Brock, H.R., 148
Brown, A.L., 122, 154
Brown, Roger, 54
Bruhn, P., 143
Burger, C.D., 148
Burke, D., 148
Burstein, L., 127, 155

C

Campbell, E.Q., 154
Campione, J.C., 122, 154
Cantor, N., 154
Carson, S., 47, 144
Cattell, James, 104, 113
Cattell, R.B., 152
Cerrick, L., 146
Change, unintentional, mindful
   learning and, 16–17
Chanowitz, B., 64, 145, 156
Cheong, Y.F., 146
Children, 44, 47–48, 55
Cognition
   age, aging and, 90
   coping skills, stigmatized status
      and, 94
   correspondence with environ-
      ment, intelligence and, 101,
      104, 107
Cognitive commitments, premature,
   92
Cognitive stage, in learning new
   skill, 26–27
Coleman, J.S., 154
Collins, A., 153–54
Competition, 57, 136

Concentration. *See* Attention/atten-
tiveness
Conditional learning
versus absolute, 19–20
memory as function of, 79–81
Condoor, S.S., 148
Context(s)
ADHD, novelty and paying
attention in, 46
ambiguity, right answers and,
133–35
basic skills, doubt and, 15–22
delayed gratification and, 57–59
drawing distinctions and, 75, 79,
81
information, presentation and,
70–71
mindless memory and, 88–89
outcomes and, 121–22
sideways learning, basic skills
and, 23
Control
coping strategies, experiment in,
128–30
decision making, experiment in,
5
perception and, 100, 101–2, 108
predictions and, 123, 128
Cox, J., 143
Craik, F., 146
Crane, M., 147
Creativity
knowledge, effect on performance, 85–86
uncertainty, right answers and,
130–33
Cripe, F.F., 46, 144
Critical thinking, 133
Culture
aging, attitudes toward, 93–97

categories of work and play and,
61–62
myths/fairy tales and, 1–2
Curriculum, 2, 127
Cutler, S., 148

D

Darwin, C., 104, 152
Davis, D., 150–51
Deci, E., 144
Decision making, 5
Delaying gratification
all work and no play, 52–56
learning myth about, 2, 6, 51–52
turning play into work, 56–59
turning work into play, 59–66
DeMay, Douglas, 26
DePaulo, B.M., 155
DeRivera, J., 155
Detterman, D.K., 153
Disability, functioning as ability,
138–39
Distinction(s)
advantages, other, 65
as alternative to rote memoriza-
tion, 75–81
making novel, conformity and,
63–64
mindful alertness to, 23
work tasks and, 60–61
Distraction, 46, 49. *See also* Atten-
tion/attentiveness
Diversity, mindfulness and, 98
Dixon, R.A., 152
Domain-specific intelligence, 106–7
Doubt, mindful learning of basic
skills and, 15–22
Douglas, Stephen, 79

Dror, I., 85, 147
Dudkin, D., 18, 141
Duncker, K., 148
Dweck, Carol, 157

E

Eck, J., 80, 147
Education
    ambiguity, multiple perspectives,
        stability and, 133–35
    basic skills and, 12
    context-free information and, 70
    intelligence, desirable outcomes
        and, 120–22
    labeling students, intelligence
        tests and, 136–37
    linear versus mindful problem
        solving, 111–15
    mindsets/myths about learning,
        2–7
    relevance in, 74–75
    sideways learning, basic skills
        and, 22–28
    socioeconomic status, students'
        achievement and, 126–27
Edwards, B., 155
Elderly. *See* Age, aging
Environment
    individual's optimum fit with,
        intelligence and, 106–7,
        137–39
    perceptions of, intelligence and,
        100–107, 115
    self-definition, mindfulness and,
        136
Epstein, J.L., 146
Equality of Educational Opportunity
    (report), 126–27

Estes, W.K., 148
Evolution, intelligence and, 104,
    105
Experience
    individual, versus group data,
        127–29
    self-definition and mindfulness,
        135–37
    sideways learning, basic skills
        and, 24–25
    stages of, acquisition of a new
        skill and, 25–27
    uncertainty, creative thought and
        right answers, 130–33, 135
Expert's perspective, right answers
    and, 120, 122–30
Eysenck, H.J., 152–53

F

Facts
    assumptions about, 19–20, 71
    conditional teaching, doubt and,
        15–16
    mindless memory and, 88–89
    as truth, 130
Fairy tales/myths, learning and,
    1–7
Feldman, D., 142
Fischhoff, B., 153
Fisher, J.D., 155
Fisher, K.B., 154
Focusing. *See* Attention/attentive-
    ness
Ford, M., 46, 143
Forgetting
    knowledge, effect on creative per-
        formance, 85–86
    learning myth about, 2

memory, mindless, dangers of, 87–89
memory and aging, 90–98
provokes mindfulness, 89–90
sleeper effect, source credibility and, 86–87
usefulness of, 83–85
Freedman, I., 144
Frensch, P.A., 153, 154
Frost, Robert, 54
 Two Tramps in Mud Time, 53
Furth, H., 151

G

"g" factor, cognitive ability, 101
Galileo, 134
Galton, Francis, 113
Galton, Sir Francis, 104
Gardner, H., 101, 121, 151, 153
Gender, learning skills and, 21–22
Genetics/heredity, 25, 104, 108
Glanzer, M., 149
Goleman, D., 151
Gould, Glenn, 27
Grams, A., 148
Gratification. *See* Delaying gratification
Greene, D., 144
Greenwald, A.G., 148
Grimm, the brothers, 93
 Four Artful Brothers, The, 120
 Hansel and Gretel, 67–68
 Three Languages, The, 35
Gross, M., 143
Group data, versus individual experience, 127–29
Guilford, J.P., 135, 155
Gurtman, M., 91, 149

H

Hall, S., 150
Harbluk, J.L., 148
Hecht, H., 148
Heller, J., 144
Helmholtz, Hermann von, 101, 102, 151
Henriksen, L., 143
Heredity. *See* Genetics/heredity
Higgins, P., 150
Hilgard, E., 146
Hochberg, J., 103, 109 (Fig.)
Holland, C., 149
Holmes, J., 144
Holson, C.J., 154
Horn, J., 151
Humphries, T., 149, 150
Hyperactivity, 46
Hypothesis testing, 122, 123

I

Ideas, stages of adopting, 3–4
Ignorance, intelligent, 112
Ikels, C., 149, 150
Images, attentiveness and, 38–39, 43, 49
Imber, L., 17, 141
Inference making, 122
Information. *See also* Facts; Rote memorization
mindful learning and, 76
mindfulness and, 4, 111
overlearned, 71, 88
reducing and organizing, as basic skill, 12
unconditional, mindless learning and, 16–18

Intelligence
  assumptions, 127
  learning myths about, 2, 100–101
  mindful problem solving, versus
    linear, 111–15
  mindfulness, alternative ability,
    107–9, 111, 138–39
  mindfulness, self-definition and,
    135–37
  mindfulness and, differences
    between, 110 (Table)
  optimum fit, individual and envi-
    ronment, 106–7, 137–39
  outcomes and, 120–23
  theories of, nineteenth century,
    101–6
Intelligence testing, 104, 105–6,
    122, 136, 137–38
Intelligent ignorance, 112
Irvine, S.H., 152

J

Jacobs, L., 150
Jacobson, L., 151
James, W., 38, 107, 114, 153
Janis, I., 36, 142, 154
Jellison, J.M., 145
Jensen, A.R., 120, 152, 153
Johansson, B., 148
Johnson, B., 149
Jones, E., 153, 154

K

Kahneman, D., 153, 154
Kepler, Johannes, 134
Kihlstrom, J.F., 154

King, C.A., 143
Kirker, W., 147
Kite, M., 149
Kolligar, J., 156
Kramer, D.A., 152
Kruglanski, A., 144
Kuiper, N., 147

L

Lamb, Charles, *Work*, 56
Landau, S., 46, 143
Langer, Ellen J., 141, 142, 143, 144,
    145, 147, 149, 153, 154, 155,
    156, 157
Larson, Gary, 58
Learners
  basic skills, 12
  labeling, intelligence tests and,
    136
  overlearned skills and, 14
  socioeconomic status, achieve-
    ment and, 126–27
Learning. *See also* Mindful learning
  conditional, 19–20, 79–81
  forgetting/memory and, 85
  mindsets/myths about, 2–7
  as re-imagining the world,
    137–39
  sideways, basic skills and, 22–28
Leippe, M.R., 148
Lepper, M., 144
Lerner, M., 144
LeVine, R., 61, 145
Levy, B., 93, 143, 150
Lichenstein, S., 154
Lichtman, R., 156
Lieberman, M., 77, 78, 147
Light, L., 148

Linear problem solving, versus
 mindful, 111–15
Liu, T., 148
Llorens Torres, Luis, *Psalms*, 83
Lorch, E.P., 143
Lou, H.C., 143

M

MacIver, D.J., 146
Maier, N.R.F., 147
Marcus, A., 62–63, 145
Markus, H., 73, 146, 147
Marquis, D.G., 146
McLachlan, D.R., 148
McPartland, J., 154
Meditation, 39, 138
Memory. *See also* Forgetting; Rote
 memorization
  age, aging and, 90–98
  aging and, alternative views of,
   93–98
  attentiveness and, 41–42, 48–49
  conditional learning, as function
   of, 79–80
  mindless, dangers of, 87–89
  usefulness of, 84
Menuhin, Yehudi, 27
Mere exposure effect, 64–65
Methylphenidate (Ritalin), 45
Milgram, S., 20, 61, 141
Milich, R., 143
Miller, D., 144
Miller, M.D., 154
Mindful attention, 41, 44
Mindful learning
  basic skills and, 15–22
  characteristics of, 4–6, 87
  drawing distinctions and, 76

perspective and, 136–39
 rote memorization, as alternative
  to, 73–75
 textbooks and, 28–31
Mindful movement, hypothesis of,
 in ADHD, 46–49
Mindfulness
  actor/observer and other perspectives, right answers and,
   123–29
  concept of, 4, 76, 111, 137–39
  context, right answers and, 135
  diversity provokes, 98
  forgetting provokes, 89–90
  intelligence and, 107–9, 110
   (Table), 111, 137–39
  linear problem solving versus,
   111–15
  mere exposure effect and, 64–65
  psychological states of, 23
  self-definition and, 135–37
  sideways learning and, 23
  uncertainty, creative thought and
   right answers, 130–33
Mindfulness (book), 4, 19
Mindlessness
  context-free information, processing of, 70–71
  defined, 4
  examples of, 4–5
  memory and, 87–89
  overlearned skills, 13
  unconditional information, learning and, 16–19
Mindset(s)
  about learning, myths and, 2–7
  about memory decline, 90
  about work and play, 53, 61–62
  premature cognitive commitments, 92

Möbius strip, 109
Monty, R.A., 155
Mood, A., 154
Moore, B., 148
Mostofsky, D.I., 103 (Fig.), 109 (Fig.)
Movement and mindfulness hypothesis in ADHD, 46–49
Mozart, Wolfgang Amadeus, 27
Mueller, C., 79, 147
Multiple intelligences, theory of, 121
Myths/fairy tales, learning and, 1–7

N

Nadler, A., 155
Natural selection, 105, 108
Navratilova, Martina, 14
Neurolinguistic programming, 26
Neurotransmitters, 45
New York Times, 4
New York Times Magazine, 141
Newstead, S.E., 152
Nisbett, R., 144, 153
Noice, H., 145, 147
Nordahl, T.E., 143
Novelty
    attentiveness and, 39, 40–43, 46, 48, 49
    mindful openness to, 23
    problem solving and, 113

O

Observer/actor, and other perspectives, right answers and, 122–29

Okakura, Kakuzo, 139
Optical illusions, 104, 109
Outcomes, intelligence and, 120–23
Overlearned information, 71, 88
Overlearned skills, 11–14, 17

P

Padden, C., 149, 150
Palmore, E., 148
Paradigm shift, 3
Park, K., 155–56
Paying attention. *See* Attention/attentiveness
Payzant, G., 142
Perception
    attentiveness and, 38
    automatic organization of, 102–4, 103 (Fig.), 109 (Fig.)
    environment, intelligence theories and, 100–106, 108
Perdue, C., 91, 149
Performance
    creative, effect of knowledge on, 85–86
    memory/memorization and, 73, 96–97
    novelty, attentiveness and, 49
    overlearned skills and, 14, 18
    technique, practice and, 24–25
Perlmuter, L.C., 155
Perret, Y.M., 143
Perspective(s)
    actor/observer and others, right answers and, 123–29
    awareness of differing/multiple, 4, 23, 76, 111, 133–35
    information, presentation and, 71, 81

varying, attentiveness and, 42–43, 48, 49
Phillips, L.D., 153
Pierce, A., 142
Pierce, R., 142
Pietrasz, L., 21, 62, 142, 145
Piper, Alison, 19
Pittman, T., 144
Play. *See* Delaying gratification
Poe, V., 143
Practice. *See* Basic skills
Pratkanis, A.R., 148
Predictions, actor/observer and others, right answers and, 123–30
Prejudice, 74–75
Premature cognitive commitments, 92
Present, mindful orientation to, 23, 89
Principle of universal development, 105
Problem solving
    intelligence as ability for, 120, 123
    linear versus mindful, 111–15
Proffitt, D.R., 148
Psychometric (intelligence) testing, 104, 105

R

Rabbit, P., 149
Radin, Dean, 4
Rapport, M.D., 143
Raudenbush, S.W., 146
Reality, external, intelligence theory and, 100–101, 107

Reder, L., 145
Relevance, learning and, 74–75, 77, 79
Remembering. *See* Forgetting; Memory
Repetition, 57
Rewards, delayed gratification and, 5–6, 53–57
Right answers
    actor/observer and other perspectives, 123–30
    ambiguity and, 133–35
    learning myth about, 2, 6, 117–20
    outcomes and, 120–23
    uncertainty, creative thought and, 129–32
Rissenberg, M., 149
Ritalin (methylphenidate), 45
Rodin, J., 149
Rogers, T., 147
Rosenthal, R., 151
Rote memorization
    drawing distinctions, as alternative to, 75–81
    information, keeping available, 73–75
    information, locking up, 69–73
    learning myth about, 2, 6, 67–69
Rowan, B., 146
Rutherford, F.J., 146
Ryan, E., 148

S

Saegart, S.C., 145
Saint-Exupéry, A. de, 141
    Little Prince, The, 9–10

Salinas, K.C., 146
Scardamalia, M., 146
Schacter, D.L., 148
Schank, R., 154, 157
Schumann, Robert, 27
Schwartz, G.E., 155
Self-esteem, mindfulness and,
    135–37
Self-reference effect, 74–75
Sher, A., 150
Sherod, D., 148
Shih, M., 47–48, 144
Sideways learning, 22–28
Siladi, N., 147
Skills, learning. *See also* Basic skills
    intelligence and, 121–23
    overlearned, 11–14, 17
    stages of experience in, 26–27
Sleeper effect, 86–87
Sloboda, John, 142
Slovic, P., 153
Smith, E.E., 153
Snow, S., 58, 145
Socioeconomic status, students'
    achievement and, 126–27
Soft vigilance, attentiveness and,
    43–44
Source credibility, 86–87
Southall, J.P.C., 151
Spearman, C., 101, 151
Spencer, H., 104, 105, 152
Spitzer, L., 149
Staub, E., 155
Steele, C.M., 57, 144, 155
Sternberg, R.J., 152, 153, 154, 156
Stimuli, unfamiliar, increased expo-
    sure to, 63–64
Students. *See* Learners
Survival, intelligence and, 105, 115

T

Tarcher, J.P., 155
Taylor, S.E., 156
Teaching. *See* Education
Testing. *See* Intelligence testing
Textbooks, mindful learning and,
    28–31
Thau, Amy, 48
Thorndike, E.L., 105, 152
Top-down teaching method, 22
Tracking, selective, 127
Training. *See* Education
Tursky, B., 155
Tversky, A., 153, 154
Twain, Mark, *Adventures of Huckle-
    berry Finn*, 60

U

Uncertainty
    basic skills, doubt and, 15–22
    creative thought and right
        answers, 130–33
Unconditional information, 88,
    92
Underwood, B., 148
Unit of analysis, 127
Universal development, principle of,
    105

V

Vigilance, soft, attentiveness and,
    43–44
Vogel, E., 150
Vyse, S.A., 143

W

Wang Ken, *Song of Joy*, 66
Waterfield, R., 28, 142
Weinfeld, E.D., 154
Weinman, C., 147, 149
Whitmore, Paul, 26
Wilcox, S., 150
Wills, T.A., 155
Wolfer, J., 36, 142, 154
Wolman, B.B., 152, 155
Wood, J., 156
Work. *See* Delaying gratification
Wrong answers. *See* Right answers

Y

Yarbus, A.L., 142
York, R.L., 154
Yuker, H.E., 156

Z

Zajonc, R., 145
Zametkin, A.J., 143
Zarit, S., 148
Zeevi, G., 144
Zentall, S.S., 46, 144

About the Author

Ellen J. Langer is Professor of Psychology at Harvard University. The recipient of a Guggenheim Fellowship, Professor Langer is author of approximately 100 journal articles and chapters in scholarly works. She is author of *Personal Politics* (with Carol Dweck), *The Psychology of Control*, and *Mindfulness*, which has been published in ten countries. She has also edited *Higher Stages of Development* with Charles Alexander and *Beliefs, Attitudes and Decision Making* with Roger Schank. In 1988 she received the Award for Distinguished Contributions to Psychology in the Public Interest from the American Psychological Association. In 1996 she received the Award for Distinguished Contributions in Basic Science to the Application of Psychology from the Association of Applied and Preventive Psychology.